KEN LANGFORD

THE MAKING OF A
CANOE SLALOM COACH

Note for Librarians: A cataloguing record for this book is available from Library and Archives Canada at www.collectionscanada.ca/amicus/index-e.html
ISBN 1-4251-0769-9

Printed in Victoria, BC, Canada. Printed on paper with minimum 30% recycled fibre.
Trafford's print shop runs on "green energy" from solar, wind and other environmentally-friendly power sources.

TRAFFORD
PUBLISHING™
Offices in Canada, USA, Ireland and UK

Book sales for North America and international:
Trafford Publishing, 6E–2333 Government St.,
Victoria, BC V8T 4P4 CANADA
phone 250 383 6864 (toll-free 1 888 232 4444)
fax 250 383 6804; email to orders@trafford.com
Book sales in Europe:
Trafford Publishing (UK) Limited, 9 Park End Street, 2nd Floor
Oxford, UK OX1 1HH UNITED KINGDOM
phone +44 (0)1865 722 113 (local rate 0845 230 9601)
facsimile +44 (0)1865 722 868; info.uk@trafford.com
Order online at:
trafford.com/06-2527

10 9 8 7 6 5 4 3 2

ACKNOWLEDGEMENTS

As the reader shares my recollections of a life in canoe slalom that has enabled me to travel the world and meet individuals, each of whom would have their own fascinating story to tell, it will bec me clear that the help, support and inspiration of many people made my journey possible;- the willingness of my father to lend me his car in the early days of travelling to events, the inspiration I took from friends and significant role models in the sport, the enthusiasm of my geography teacher who introduced me to a whole new world of outdoor activities before it was fashionable to do so, the patience of my work colleagues who covered my absences without complaint when I was on many trips around the world, and the educational authorities who allowed them to do so. My wife and family have been totally supportive, and I have been guilty of taking advantage of that fact on many occasions as I searched for ways to satisfy my competitive instincts. There are so many people who have been inspirational role models without realising it. To each and all of these I am grateful.

However, I would like to dedicate this book to certain individuals close to me who showed that, even in adversity, a positive approach to life is the best way to survive.

As has been said many times – "Whether you think you can or can't do something, you are probably right!"

INTRODUCTION

When I started paddling in 1960, the sport of canoe slalom was still in its infancy. Many of those who had taken part in the early world championships were still active paddlers – although many had also moved on to take organisational and administrative responsibility as well. The early pioneers, including Jack Spuhler, Bill Crockett, Bill Goodman and his wife Heather, were people I knew well, and from whom I gleaned much information about the growth of the sport. Through conversation, I believe I understood something of their beliefs, values and hopes for the future of the sport. The early days were very much focused on enjoyment and participation. Prizes, medals and other extrinsic rewards seemed to be much less important than the satisfaction of mastering skills and developing competences. These individuals were, in the main, **true** amateurs, who were not depressed because they lost competitions. Winning, as it has taken me many years to realise, is not the aim, even though success is appreciated by us all! The fact is, winning is not within **our** control, and depends on how other people perform who are competing against us. The value of competition is in enabling us to compare **our own** performance with the demands of the course. Analysing where we make mistakes, or select the wrong option, enables us to assess our own level of competence, and determine which aspects of performance need greatest attention in training.

The role of the coach is to help in this process. He cannot help a paddler to 'win', but he can help to raise the standard of performance. In other words, winning is not a legitimate **aim.** Winning is the **reward** for performing well.

I suppose, on reflection, that I always understood this to be true, but had never spent time reflecting on **why** I coached. Now, looking back, I believe that I had found an area which **really was** within my control.

I was competing at international level from 1963 to 1974, and represented Britain in five world championships in slalom, and two more in white water racing. I was also actively involved in coaching from 1964 until I retired from international involvement in 1996, which means that I only had two years of international competition **without** the responsibility of coaching. There had been no effective slalom coaching structure since Oliver Cock moved on to become National Coach (non competitive) in 1960, and someone had to do it! Perhaps my unique involvement in the sport is reflected in my participation in the 1973 World Championships at Muotathal. At this event, I was Slalom Team Coach, International Judge, National Team Manager, and, in this capacity, responsible for redesigning the top section of the course before practice runs after the river suddenly rose and washed out the original course. I was also competing in the slalom individual and team events, and managed to finish in 16th place! I think that counts as total involvement.

The opinions and recollections are mine. So too, are any mistakes. The emphasis given to certain situations might reflect events as I would like them to have been, or were significant and memorable to me at the time! Hopefully this is not the case. I have tried to be as accurate as I can, and hope that others will be able to share some great memories.

* * * *

From its earliest beginnings, coaching in canoe slalom has had a chequered past. At times, results in international competition have been brilliant but, like all sports, there have been periods of mediocrity when success has eluded the teams sent abroad to represent Great Britain.

There is no direct relationship between the quality of coaching and international success although performances and international success have improved at the same time as a structured coaching system has evolved. In the embryonic beginnings of the sport at the first world championships – below the main weir in Geneva in 1949, the British team took three of the last four places. The next four championships, 1951 to 1957, saw only two paddlers place outside the bottom third on the results sheet. In 1955 and 1957 two ladies competed but failed to get out of the bottom three places on either occasion. Even though the British team of Keith White, Paul Farrant and Ian Carmichael won the team event at an international event in Lipstadt in northern Germany in 1958, it was a total surprise to most other nations when Paul Farrant became Britain's first world champion in 1959 on the same weir course in Geneva where the inaugural event had been held.

One who was less surprised than most was Farrant himself who had given up his career in business, temporarily, and taken a job with Thames Conservancy, which enabled him to canoe from home to work along the river and train on the Thames weirs as he made his way home. This regime was enhanced when he took lodgings in the lead-up to the 1959 championships with Oliver Cock who, for many years, was the national coach of the British Canoe Union, and whose house backed onto the river at Henley on Thames. This made an ideal training environment and probably accounted for the success of both Farrant and Ian Carmichael who also trained on the Thames and who finished in 14th place in those championships. The pair were the first British paddlers to make the top half in a world championship event. Paul Farrant tragically died in a road accident in 1960. In his memory, the

BCU commissioned the **Paul Farrant Trophy** and donated it to the International Canoe Federation. This trophy, awarded to the winner of the men's kayak singles, did not return to Britain until 1977 – but more of that later. Ian Carmichael continued to paddle and, in 1961, came 19th in Dresden behind Keith White (11th). For the second time Britain had two competitors in the top half at a world championships.

Oliver Cock, as National Coach of the B.C.U. was not only the slalom team coach, but also spent much of his time travelling the length and breadth of Britain promoting participation, health and safety, and generally increasing the profile of the sport. However, his support of Paul Farrant, and the offer of a superb training environment for a championship event that was to be held in the unique environment of a weir (with its boils and eddies and without the natural river features of rocks and falls), was a major departure from the typical preparation that had occurred in the past. In short, it showed what was possible with a structured approach to training.

So why was this basic lesson not learnt by performers in earlier years? For many years, I, as a coach, failed to understand the concept of taking part, performing 'so badly', and then not doing anything about it. After all, did not Vince Lombardi say that "winning is not the most important thing; it is the only thing"? Looking back now, it was more a case of ignorance on my part and did not begin to make sense until I competed in the New York Marathon several years later finishing 6,286[th]. I did not think I had done 'badly'. I had given everything, and had a great sense of achievement and considerable satisfaction. I achieved **my** goal. I do not know how many of those early competitors came away with a feeling of satisfaction. I am unable to look inside their heads. Therefore, how could I judge whether they under-performed or not without a knowledge of their personal goals?

By 1963, Carmichael and White had retired and the British Team comprised a much younger and less experienced squad. At 20 years old, only Martin Rohleder remained from the 1961 team and was joined by world championship 'novices' including Dave

Mitchell who was to remain dominant until his retirement from slalom after the 1972 Olympic Games. The West German coach, Stephan Koerner, referred to them as the 'young boys' because of their inexperience. The individual performances were less than spectacular with only Mitchell in the top half, but in the team event he, along with Martin Rohleder and Geoff Dinsdale, came away with a bronze medal.

* * * *

Looking back, I suppose I was a bit of a loner and left primary school not really knowing many of my classmates. This was not helped by missing the last four weeks at the school. I had to be kept away because my sister had german measles and the whole family were in 'quarantine' so that the infection could be contained in the family. I was one of a handful of pupils in my class to pass the 'eleven plus' exam and go to a grammar school, and I was the only one to move to Manchester Central Grammar which was a short walk from Piccadilly Station in the centre of the city. It was a thriving and exciting place to be and added to my independence. It was my geography teacher 'Jos' Horrocks who got me interested in the 'great outdoors' by organising a trip from Manchester to Hayfield culminating in a trek up to Kinder Downfall in the Peak District of Derbyshire. The National Park had been created only five years earlier in 1949 and this was a totally new experience. Subsequent trips to Edale and Buxton and further away by coach to the Lake District opened up a new way of life that became irresistible. I joined the local Boy Scouts and was quite successful, being one of the youngest in Manchester to become a Queens Scout, the top award in scouting. I became assistant Scoutmaster and, at about the same time, I left school to work in a bank in the city centre. School leavers from my grammar school generally went into banking, accountancy, or insurance or some other job in the city. It was quite a small percentage who went to university.

It was while working in my first post, a bank in Moss Side, that I went to a 'hobbies exhibition' in December 1960 at the City Hall on Liverpool Road in the city centre. Manchester Canoe Club had a stand and was showing films of Scottish rivers paddled during the previous summer. The club ran two 'swimming pool' sessions each week at the New Islington Baths off Great Ancoats Street and were inviting new members to come along and join. I was seventeen, had just learned to drive and was able to borrow my father's car and went the following week. Little did he realise at the time that the mileage on that car would treble over the next few years as I 'borrowed' it most weekends to travel the length and breadth of the country There were two pools, one for beginners and an 'experts' pool for those who could eskimo roll and wanted to train on the three 'gates' suspended above the water. It was always fairly crowded with up to a dozen canoes sprinting the length of the pool – good preparation, although I did not realise it at the time, for the free practice at slalom events prior to the introduction of organised practice runs.

Manchester Canoe Club was really a 'postal' club and drew members from across the country because the secretary, Maurice Rothwell, was also secretary of the National Slalom Committee. Anyone who competed for Great Britain, or who had aspirations in that direction, joined the club to keep in touch with developments on the national and international scene. In the 1960's, membership approached two hundred. Without realising it, I had joined the top club in the sport. Paddlers such as Julian Shaw (national champion) and Nigel Morley (international competitior) trained at times in the pool with everyone else. This was when I first met Martin Rohleder. He was already an international performer and I had not even been in a slalom kayak! From my earliest involvement in the sport these were my role models. More importantly, they were the only comparisons I had when it came to analysing my own performance. They were instrumental, without even knowing it, in my ambition to master this sport. I think I even aspired to paddle like Martin Rohleder simply because he was the same age as myself!

By February 1961, I had been moved to a small sub-branch in Trafford Park with only the manager and myself in the bank. I like to think I had been spotted for possible promotion but I have no reason to believe this was actually true. The reality of this move was that sometimes I left work at 3.15.p.m. and sometimes at 7.00.p.m. It all depended how long it took to balance the books at the end of the day. As a serious and committed slalomist (of a full two months experience!) this work was interfering with my ambitions to get to the standard of those who trained with me! My father was working in the Civil Service in Manchester and, not only did he have regular hours, he had 'flexi-time' which allowed him to start and finish earlier – as long as he did the requisite number of hours. I wanted some of this and joined the Inland Revenue shortly afterwards.

My training was far more regular now. I trained on the Bridgewater Canal, paddling fourteen miles twice a week, did two 'baths sessions each week, did circuit training and weight training at the city centre YMCA in the lunch hour and spent weekends away on rivers in Wales and the Pennines. I was ready for my first Division Four slalom competition and entered Swarkestone slalom on the Trent above Nottingham in July 1961. No-one had helped me with my training. Slalom coaches did not exist. I just watched others and read a few books; but I **was** ready.

Arriving at Swarkestone with my new folding kayak (all kayaks had to be folding at that time), I realised that, despite all my hours of training, I had done no training with slalom gates on moving water. I was fairly fit and spent several hours in the melee of the 'free practice' time before the event trying to remedy this situation. In the competition I had a reasonable time, clocked up too many penalties, and finished fourteenth. Other club members congratulated me on the result but I believed these were more in the way of commiserations. In my eyes, I had failed and went away very disappointed but even more determined to put things right before my next event. I was certainly not going to enter any more events without adequate preparation. I did not enter another event until March 1962 at Sandford Lock on the

Thames near Oxford but I spent many winter weekends on club trips to the Dee, Ribble and other rivers in the north of England, often suspending single poles from overhanging trees and practising breaking into eddies while descending rapids. Inevitably, boat control improved and, because the canvas hull was easily punctured by rocks near the surface, ability to 'read' the water became a priority if hours of boat repairs were to be avoided.

I **really** was ready for the Sandford lock slalom and even passed two other competitors on the course during my runs. Although a competitor was required to give way if caught up by a faster paddler, it caused confusion for the organisers who gave me one of the slowest times. I was already on my way home by the time the results were publicised and had no idea what to do, or how to make a protest. It was actually too late in any case.

The following month, everything came together. Following a fourth place in the Division Four slalom at Shepperton, a win the next weekend at Marsh Lock, Henley on Thames earned me promotion to Division Three. Both these events were significant – being on weir courses that many 'northerners' disliked. For me they had the atmosphere of ampitheatres with the spectators and other competitors close to the action. This was not the case on the longer and more open river courses. The following week, I won promotion at Bevere on the Severn, and two weeks later I came second in Division Two at Thistlebrig rapids on the River Tay near Perth. Two more tenth places in Division Two at Llandyssul and Builth Wells earned me promotion to Division One, the top division, at the end of that year. I had come a long way since Sandford Lock and felt I had a lot to do during the closed season if I was to be prepared and do justice to myself in 1963.

Training increased. I got permission to leave a boat at Sale Cruising Club, a canal cruising group who had moorings on the Bridgewater Canal next to Brooklands railway station. I could now do my 14 mile paddle three times each week. I continued with swimming, weight training and circuit training at the YMCA and even started playing volleyball. The weekends were reserved for river trips. I had met Dave Mitchell, the 'new kid on the block' at the Llandyssul Division Two slalom when I was competing. He was competing in Division One. Both divisions were held on the same course at that time – with Division Two missing out a couple of the gates that were perceived to be more difficult. More time was spent training at Chester on the weir where Mitchell trained. The Dee was much cleaner than any river in the Manchester area and the odd time I did venture onto Northenden weir on the Mersey the height of the foam suds prevented any serious training.

1962 was the winter of the big freeze and canoeing was curtailed for two months. Ice skating on the Dee at Chester and in Liverpool replaced canoeing for a time. The activity of 'canogganing' was born where we used canoes as toboggans and slid down snow covered slopes using the paddle to turn the boat sideways. Then, by pressing the blades into the snow on the downhill side we could perform airborne eskimo rolls at speed.

Easter came and it was the first slalom of the year at Grandtully on the River Tay. I had done as much training as anyone. The event was won by Martin Rohleder. I finished in second place. I had come close to beating the person who had first inspired me a little over two years earlier. Nobody was more surprised than I. I knew I had trained hard but never expected to be so successful in my first event in the top division.

The Selection and Executive Committees of the BCU Slalom Committee met immediately after the event to choose the team for the 1963 world championships that were to be held at Spittal in the Karnten district of Austria. Performance in the Grandtully slalom was an important pointer for selection. My 'one off' performance was not enough to earn selection. I had no track record and nobody knew how I would cope with the experience and pressure of a world championship. Understandably, I was not chosen. However, I was selected to compete at my first international event at Monschau in Germany. I had progressed from Division Four to international competitor in just twelve months and went on to finish 20th at Monschau.

It would be nice to attribute my rapid rise in the sport to

some phenomenal talent that was lurking within. Reality is much different. There were several factors, some accidental and some more deliberate.

Even at the age of ten, I had a strong competitive instinct combined with a capacity for concentration over a long period of time. There was a field at the bottom of the road where I lived and a group of us hatched up the idea of building a 'full-size' athletics track using spades and barrows from the potting sheds at the bottom of the various back gardens. A circuit of the finished track was probably thirty or forty yards at most and consisted of mud because, for some incomprehensible reason, we had removed all the grass! I do not know why, but we never raced against each other. Maybe there was a fear of being shown up. Instead, we just tried to see who could do the most laps which meant the person with the most perseverance carried on and told white lies about the number of laps completed. Nobody actually cared and the grass gradually grew back as we lost interest in the project after a couple of weeks.

On one occasion, I remember cycling the thirty miles to Chester at the age of 12 or 13 with a couple of friends. The time taken was not as important as completing the journey without stopping for a rest. We believed that if we stopped just once it would be harder to start again and 'rest stops' would become even more frequent. I used the same strategy when taking part in the London Marathon thirty years later! Pushing myself for long periods of time on my own was essential for the long hours of continuous paddling on the canal and I steadily improved in goal setting and the long term planning of training in the closed season. 'Giving in' was failure – especially when the goal was important. Boredom was seldom an issue.

The importance of the training environment cannot be understated. I had joined the most successful club in the country but, not knowing any different, I assumed that all clubs were more or less like Manchester. From the start, I had trained with the best paddlers, and had role models on which to base long term goals – even if they were only aspirations or dreams at the time. The

14

combination of role models, an ability to work with determination and a high degree of intensity towards long term goals, and a basic enjoyment of all the factors associated with the sport proved effective enough to cancel any need to compare my performance with others. For me, it really was competition against the course in the same way that I had accepted the challenge of climbing hills and mountains of the Lake District and Snowdonia.

From the beginning of my competitive years in slalom, I think that, subconsciously, I understood the coaching principle – 'Winning is **not** the aim. Getting it right is the aim. Winning is the prize for getting it right!' In other words, winning depends on the performance of other people. I might win if they perform badly or lose if they perform well. In either case, the outcome is beyond my control, whereas I **am** in control of my own performance and the aim should be to get that right. There are many different and equally effective regimes and coaching environments that improve standards of performance. Many successful athletes attribute success to the degree of 'head to head' sessions in training or competition. Rowing, for example, brings out the greatest effort from crews when they are 'neck and neck' approaching the finishing line. Middle distance running often employs 'pacemakers' to draw more from the runners as they seek new championship records. Canoe slalom is different. No comparison with other paddlers is possible **during** the competitive run and, therefore, no incentive exists to put on an extra spurt to catch up or break away. When times are compared, it is too late to do anything about it. For the slalomist, the only logical approach is to execute each run in accordance with a well thought out plan.

* * * *

The second Division One slalom of 1963 was held at Hambleden Weir below Henley on Thames. This was the home of Chalfont Park Canoe Club, the top slalom club of the nineteen fifties, who still have their club house on a small island in the river immediately below the weir. The club had run its first Shepperton slalom as early as 1951. Four of the seven paddlers in the 1953 world championships, including Paul Farrant, came from the club. Mary Farrant, Paul's sister and the 1954 British ladies champion, was the first lady (with Heather Goodman from the Lake District) to compete in a world championships for Britain. The year was 1955. Paul had been British champion in 1953 and 1959 when championships were decided on one designated event. (It was from 1961 onwards that a series of events during the year was used to determine national champions). As a training venue, Hambleden was excellent. Frequently, a group of us from Manchester would drive down on a Friday night and camp on the island that was reached in a small punt. During a weekend we could have four or five one hour gate sessions and disappear into Henley for the evenings.

By 1963, the famous Hambleden wave that enabled paddlers to surf across it and develop rough water skills had disappeared because of engineering work on the weir. However, it was possible to use the full length of the weir and design a course of over 200 seconds – twice as long as Marsh Lock or Shepperton. Although both of us had numerous penalties, I did finally beat Martin Rohleder by one place – finishing sixth.

* * * *

Monschau is a small town on the border between Germany and Belgium and was my first international. Following the slalom at Grandtully, all paddlers who had been selected for internationals stayed behind for a 'team meeting'. Jack Spuhler, who had competed for Britain in the first world championships in 1949, addressed us all. Jack was one of the major players in the establishment of the sport on the international stage. Born in Geneva, he was fluent in French, German and English which were the three languages of the International Canoe Federation. He was a naturalised British subject and much of the early documentation of the federation was translated by him into the three official languages. He knew everything! Firstly, we were given a grant of £10 (or was it £15? I'm not sure now.) £5 was taken back to pay for our tracksuits which we could collect four weeks later. We were warned about the markings in the centre of Belgian roads which put different restrictions on where we could or could not overtake. Finally, we were told to sort out our own transport arrangements, make the cross channel ferry bookings, and to be in the Monschau campsite the night before the competition. Then, after fifteen minutes and good luck wishes, we dispersed.

In a weird sort of way the brevity of the meeting filled me with confidence. Here was a man who was at the pinnacle of the sport but who felt no need to speak to us for more than fifteen minutes before sending us off to a foreign country – only my second time abroad. Nothing was said about the actual competition. He trusted us and I felt good. At times ignorance really is bliss!

The river was only 10 metres wide and ran through the centre of this small town at the bottom of a limestone gorge. Artificial pools had been created on the course using scaffold planks to raise the water level, and the river flow was controlled by a large dam five miles above the town. The course was very like those at Llandyssul on the Teifi or the River Lune in low water. The piped 'beerkeller' music gave the whole place a festive atmosphere that added to the occasion when masses of spectators came to watch. This was totally different from the handful of spectators that we were used to at events in Britain.

Finishing 20th was very satisfying at the time and I felt I had justified my selection.

* * * *

One of the reasons for the success of Manchester Canoe Club was the driving force of Maurice Rothwell. His family owned and ran Rothwell's Brewery company which was taken over by Marstons in the 1950's enabling Maurice to give all his time and energy to canoeing at local and national level. He had been a competitive rower with Agecroft Rowing Club on the River Irwell in Salford and was part of the squad in training for the 1948 Olympics. The Irwell at that time, and until the 1970's, was an open sewer running into the Manchester Ship Canal and separating the cities of Manchester and Salford. A documentary on the river, at that time, made the observation that the Irwell, in its journey through Lancashire, had expended so much energy driving the cotton mills that the ship canal was built to carry it to the sea at Liverpool! I could see the river from the ninth floor offices of the building where I worked in the Civil Service, and watched the garbage and debris floating past. I am not sure why Maurice became more involved in canoeing than in his first sport of rowing. However, he did enjoy the great outdoors and organised many river trips at home and abroad. River touring was the canoeing equivalent of the 'fartlek' training that runners did as part of their winter training for the athletics season and I have fond memories of trips in 1962 to the Lune at Sedbergh and the Nith from Sanquahar to Dumfries because, unlike the Irwell, they were so clean and unpolluted that I could see pebbles on the beds of the rivers fifteen feet beneath the surface. We swam in the rivers, performed eskimo rolls and even drank the water – although usually boiling it first! The Bridgewater canal at Sale was never as clean but, consequently, never froze if I paddled towards the city centre and Trafford Park. I am not sure if this was due to the warmer inner city air or the concoction of chemicals in the water acting as anti-freeze and taking the skin off my hands.

The two highlights of the year were the annual New Year walking weekend and the two weeks summer tour of rivers in Europe. Since I had not been selected for the world championships in 1963, I went on the summer tour which included the Vorder-Rhein (the upper Rhine) in Switzerland. The hot weather could not compensate for the freezing cold water that was the snow-melt from glaciers in the Bernese Oberland. The river had to be treated with respect because the colour of the water made it difficult to recognise wave patterns and submerged obstacles.

Everything was a milky grey caused by the suspended sediment in the melt-water. During the two weeks we managed to travel as spectators to Spittal and watched the world championships. I felt proud to be British as the team took its first team event medal but a little disappointed at not being part of it. It had not been a problem at the time of selection but I had performed well at Monschau – too late for it to matter.

Back at home the season ran its course and I finished in the top six on the rankings with Dave Mitchell as national champion – a position he held until his *first* retirement in 1967.

* * * *

Most slalom courses on natural river courses were more than four minutes in length. Grandtully was the longest at four and a half minutes. Thames weir events tended to average less than two minutes. This discrepancy in course length led to the emergence of two disparate groups of paddlers. The 'weir' paddlers at Chalfont Park, Twickenham, Shepperton and Windsor clubs thrived in the wake of Farrant's success at Geneva. Most were good exponents of eskimo rolls and could handle the turbulence and variability of the 'boily' water below the weirs. The paddlers further north were better able to read river patterns, recognise submerged rocks, shoot rapids and falls, and spent time running rivers in spate during autumn and winter. Many had an intense dislike of weir courses, regarding them as unpredictable, variable and unfair. Of course, there were paddlers who were able to excel on both types of course. Geoff Dinsdale is a good example – being a weir paddler who was in the bronze medal team on the natural river course at the Spittal world championships. In reality, the 'split' between 'weir paddlers' and 'river paddlers' was due less to dislike of certain types of course and more related to the geography of Britain. South east of a line running from Southampton to the Wash there are no significant areas of high land. The only major river systems are the Thames and the Medway which flow slowly with no significant gradient throughout their length. There was no choice for slalom paddlers but to use the rough water below weirs in this half of Britain. North west of the line, rivers in their upper courses had steeper gradients giving rise to more natural rapids which provided appropriate slalom sites. Moreover, the length of slalom courses in the nineteen sixties meant that paddlers competed in both slalom and white water racing – even at international level. The weir specialists who had performed with distinction in the nineteen fifties had been superceded by the river paddler who excelled at both slalom and whitewater racing.

In Britain, slalom is the 'summer' sport while whitewater racing takes place during the autumn and winter when river levels are higher. After the slalom season, one of the first races of the autumn was on the Usk below Brecon. I was at Dave Mitchell's house waiting for Martin Rohleder to arrive from Snowdonia on his motor bike the evening before the race so we could travel down together. Sadly his motorbike hit a farm vehicle on the A5 as he rode towards Chester from Betws y Coed. He died shortly afterwards in hospital. Three top level canoeists had died in the four years since Paul Farrant. All were on mopeds or motorbikes. I decided then that I would only travel by car. Martin's death was a major shock to the canoeing world and I took great pleasure in receiving the Rohleder trophy from his mother a few years later when I finally won the Serpents Tail slalom. The bronze trophy was donated by Manchester Canoe Club in his memory.

Two series of 'whitewater' tests were held each year. The first were monthly time trials lasting seven to ten minutes down the River Leven from below Lake Windermere to the falls at Backbarrow. Times were adjusted to take into account the river level. Bronze and Silver 'dippers' were awarded in the form of a lapel badge in the shape of the bird found on the river. The gold 'dipper' invariably went to Dave Mitchell whose explosive power in this event few could match. The second series were the Dee Races which ran from the Horseshoe Falls to the weir above the town falls in Llangollen. We could not race through the town because the main weir about a hundred metres below the town bridge was vertical and five metres high (until it was destroyed by the floods of December 1964) and considered to be unshootable in most conditions. We had shot the weir in 1963 down the salmon ladder which was a series of one metre drops built against the downstream face of the weir. Unlike the Leven tests, which took place throughout the year, the Dee Races were held in the closed season between November and February – not for any masochistic reason but because we only had access to this superb piece of training water outside the 'salmon season' that extended from February to October. On several occasions we had to break the ice around the finish area before the race could start. I seemed to have a greater tolerance of 'frozen fingers' than many paddlers, including Dave Mitchell, and won the 1963-64 series. Although this was just another part of training, there was a competitive aspect which thrived between paddlers of the various clubs that seemed to give a greater edge over the paddlers from the Thames clubs.

* * * *

By the end of 1963, I had become an established member of Manchester Canoe Club and had been elected to the committee. There was a very strong touring section. Leaders were appointed for each trip and they made all the arrangements and sought permissions from landowners and riparian owners, agreed start and finish points and arranged an appropriate campsite. I tried to stick to the competition issues. I am not sure whether it was a good move at the time but it was the beginning of my involvement in the sport *out of* the boat. The club ran several events each year including the 'Serpents Tail' slalom by the Chain Bridge in Llangollen. Club members were expected to help. Eventually, I was course designer and other people took over when I was not available. Committee members were expected to do a bit more! I learned fairly quickly that, if I was to have the necessary time to prepare for my own competition runs, I needed to do *my bit* prior to the event and joined in the course erection team – gradually playing a more important role. Soon, it was accepted that a group of the better paddlers would take a day's leave from work and erect the course before the event organisers arrived on the Friday evening, and then maintain the course throughout the weekend. I was not specifically **given** the job of course designer but usually arrived with a series of suitable sequences which the others found acceptable. Perhaps part of the reason was our practice of erecting gates for training whenever we went away for training sessions. A group of five or six paddlers were able to erect a full course in half a day and were left to 'get on with it'. If there had been complaints about the course design or the fairness of it, things might have changed, but the absence of change (or demands for change) suggests that most paddlers were satisfied.

* * * *

It was 1964, and I was now paddling in the top division, competing in slalom and whitewater racing, designing and erecting slalom courses and serving on the committee of the strongest club in the country – all without any apparent conflict of interest! Selection came again after the Grandtully Easter slalom and I was named in the team for the pre-world championships to be held in Merano, Italy, with Dave Mitchell and John Woodhouse of Chester. Training was going well – three sessions each week at the YMCA in Manchester during the lunch hour, three evening sessions on the Bridgewater Canal, pool sessions at Islington Baths, and most weekends away. The change of employment to the Civil Service was perfect in allowing me to train effectively. I was able to put in 20 hours of quality training each week (which was much more than most of my contemporaries were able or willing to manage.

The second slalom of the year at Grandtully was my first win and a good confidence boost before the trip to Italy, where we were to compete in both slalom and whitewater racing.

Merano was the site of the 1953 world championships, and

the slalom course ran through the centre of the town making it excellent for spectators and paddlers alike. It was to be the venue for the 1965 championships and so this year was the opportunity for the organisers to have a 'dress rehearsal' for the main event under the eyes of the International Canoe Federation. It also gave paddlers an idea of the conditions they would meet and afforded management the chance to select hotels, training sites, and deal with issues that might affect team preparations. In reality, the British team did not have 'management'. It had helpers such as Ian Pendleton who made up in enthusiasm for what he lacked in his understanding of the technical needs of slalomists. Few people, apart from the team members themselves, had any understanding of the training we were doing and were generally ignorant of our needs. By comparison, the East Germans, West Germans, and Czechs had very experienced coaches who were closely involved in the management and training of their paddlers. The British were **really** enthusiastic amateurs training in a way that seemed to produce improvement but without a scientific understanding of the psychology or physiology of performance. Our advantage over other teams was limited to greater understanding of rivers and their characteristics, and access to the sea where boat control was enhanced on surfing weekends. We were able to perform end over end loops as we rode the waves towards the beach and dug the nose of the boat into the back tow – or the sand! Other teams were less at home on the heavier water and some were even intimidated by it.

The whitewater event preceded the slalom. Our training on the river race course went without incident but, on the day before the race, the Austrian paddler Leitner drowned. He had apparently been unable to get out of his boat after a capsize on one of the more difficult sections. The river race was abandoned.

Because the event was a rehearsal for the following year's world championships, it was decided to proceed with the slalom but to abandon the team event as a mark of respect to the Austrian. Paddlers competed with mixed emotions and the team event prizes were awarded to the nations with the best overall scores in the individual events. Britain came third but it did not really mean anything. Leitner's death did have a positive outcome because it led to a review of safety procedures in the sport. Footrests, spraydecks and lifejackets were scrutinised at home and by the ICF. Attempts were made by some in the BCU to make slalomists wear the BCU approved lifejacket that was more suitable for open water but, because it turned the paddler onto his back (to keep his face out of the water if unconscious), was totally inappropriate for the slalomist who wanted to be on his front swimming towards the bank. The outcome was a differentiation between lifejackets and 'buoyancy aids'. The discussion had been effective in raising the issue, and manufacturers started to produce 'buoyancy aids' and safety helmets especially for slalomists. Earlier safety helmets were cyclist crash helmets made of leather. Other helmets that were available were either too heavy or filled with water when the paddler was upside down preventing him from performing an eskimo roll.

The season ended, and I had made it to number two in the rankings behind Dave Mitchell but I continued to get involved in off the water aspects of the sport including changes to rules, judging, course design, safety issues and issues associated with practice at events. These were issues brought up at the AGM of the slalom committee where, as a club representative, I probably had **too** much to say, sometimes, because I felt decisions were being taken by club representatives who I felt were 'uncompetitive slalomists' who did not understand the needs of paddlers who were training twenty or thirty hours each week. I saw them as casual organisers who put in a couple of hours each week and were not serious enough about improving the standard of competition.

I had seen, with my own eyes, the professionalism of the management teams of other nations and we were not even close. I learned much later that, although other countries were well organised at international level, slalom in Britain was probably stronger than anywhere else in the world and had greater depth.

On the way home from Merano, Dave Mitchell, John Woodhouse, Ian Pendleton and myself were invited by Werner Zimmerman to his home in Zurich where he gave us a prototype white water racing boat to bring back to Britain. Werner had been a bronze medal winner at the first world championships in 1949 and his whole family were Swiss international slalom paddlers. In fact they were the nucleus of the Swiss Team. There were no white water racing boats being produced in Britain and we were given permission to make a mould and produce a few boats 'in the interest of developing the sport in the UK'. John Woodhouse, who also designed the KW3 slalom boat that we used in the 1965 world championships, took the boat to Chester and produced a 'super-lightweight' boat which he brought to the second Dee race of the 1964/5 series in December, 1964.

After really heavy rain, the river was in full flood for the Saturday before the race (the highest level since the major floods of the nineteen forties) and Dave Mitchell, John and myself launched above the Chain Bridge Hotel. The water was very heavy and when John hit a particularly large stopper at the 'Serpents Tail' his boat broke in half behind the seat and he was forced to bale out. The speed of the current resulted in a swim of a hundred metres or so before he could reach the bank.

A bit shaken, but undeterred, we climbed into our slalom boats and paddled the two miles down to the town. Landing a fair distance above the top weir we walked into the town looking at the massive wall of water that ruled out any attempt to paddle under the bridge. Even worse was the town weir with its drop of three metres – except that it was not three metres anymore. The drop was one metre but the back-tow below the weir was twenty metres and full of logs and tree trunks being pulled upstream and smashing like battering rams into the weir.

We did not paddle again that day! The high water level resulted in cancellation of the race but the rain continued. The water authority had tried to contain the flood water in Bala Lake but on

Sunday morning was forced to contact landowners in the valley telling them to move livestock to higher ground immediately. They needed to open the sluices at Bala because there was a danger to the dam. When the water was released, the Chain Bridge Hotel (five metres above normal river level) was flooded and the river flowed both sides of the hotel. In Llangollen, the railway line was flooded and the back-tow below the weir increased to thirty metres. Inevitably, the tree trunks battering the weir from below, destroyed it. Weirs are only designed to withstand pressure from upstream!

When the waters finally subsided, the five metre weir was only one metre high and was navigable by canoe – apart from the mass of twisted metal which was all that remained of the reinforced concrete. It took the next twelve months for the river authority to clear the debris and make the site reasonably safe. We had a new slalom site that would stage its first event in 1966! The railway had already been earmarked for closure in the government's Beeching plan to reduce unprofitable routes. Damage to tracks in the area was severe and the line did not re-open after the floods.

* * * *

A major political change occurred at the end of 1964. The East Germans, as we referred to them, competed as the DDR (The German Democratic Republic) which had been acceptable in Geneva, Dresden and Spittal, where the previous three championships had taken place. Italy refused to grant visas to the DDR and, to avoid confrontation, the venue was changed from Merano to Spittal because there were no political issues with the Austrian government. The ICF were amenable to this last minute change because the organisers had just proved themselves capable of organising an event at this level. I was glad that I had watched the 1963 championships and felt I knew a little more of what to expect.

1963 was the last year of folding boats in world championships. The construction of kayaks had changed because of the introduction of fibre-glass. As early as 1960, Maurice Rothwell had built one of the first fibreglass canoes in the greenhouse conservatory on the rear of his house in Manchester. He christened it the 'Maid of St. Helens', and although it probably weighed in excess of thirty kilos he paddled it in 1962 on the River Nith in Dumfriesshire – which was one of the first tours I did with the club. Maurice was known for **always** paddling "when the river temperature got above 65º and the air temperature reached 80º". It seldom happened but that was one of the weekends!

The development of fibreglass kayaks in Britain had started in 1961 when Streamlyte Mouldings, of Brighton, (who made fibreglass motor cycle fairings) brought a fibreglass canoe to a 'hobbies exhibition'. It was very heavy and the design was inappropriate to white water paddling. The firm's owners, Roy and Gordon Staley, were introduced to Keith White who had been one of the most successful slalom paddlers of the 1950's and early 1960's. Discussions led to the production of the KW1, which was similar in design to the typical folding wood and canvas canoes but was made of fibreglass. Most importantly, it was similar in weight and 'competitive' against the folding boats currently in use.

A few paddlers, including Dave Mitchell, were using rigid canoes by the end of 1962. By 1963, apart from the small number of paddlers fighting for selection for the 1963 World Championships, most competitive paddlers were discarding folding boats in favour of rigid fibreglass canoes for slalom, and even those who were aiming for world championship selection were using fibreglass boats for British competitions.

Other countries, especially those of the former communist countries of the Eastern Bloc, were slower in developing fibreglass technology, and it was too late to change the regulations to reflect development of canoe construction in time for 1963. International competitions were held with categories for F1 (folding singles) and

R1 (rigid singles). It was something of a mockery in the world championships of that year because the West Germans competed in fibreglass kayaks that were split into sections and erected inside a canvas skin. Their innovation had changed the design of the traditional kayak – even though any perceived advantage was partially negated by an increase in weight. At the end of the year, F1 and R1 categories disappeared and were replaced by K1 (kayak singles).

* * * *

1965 was the first year when fibreglass canoes were the norm. The different rates of development and construction meant a wide range of designs were on show. The East German 'Hartung' was most reminiscent of the folding kayaks of two years earlier. It did not have a greater deal of 'rocker' (the amount of curve along the keel line). This gave it speed but necessitated leaning it over to get it to turn quickly. The West German boats had more roundly constructed edges and more 'rocker' which meant greater manoeuvrability at the expense of speed. Britain had had a variety of designs from top paddlers, that Streamlyte had put into production. For 1965, John Woodhouse, of Chester, who was in the team for the world championships, had designed the KW3 which was a low volume boat that performed well on the river courses in this country. The 1963 championships in Spittal had taken place in low water on a river with a steep gradient. The success of the team in winning a bronze medal gave us confidence as we travelled to this same venue for the 1965 championships.

* * * *

Arriving in Spittal, things were **very** different. The river was in spate and a torrent of dark grey flood water flowed down the steep sided gorge at speeds of twenty five miles an hour and more. Julian Shaw, who had been in the 1959 team at Geneva, was team manager. Dave Mitchell, John Woodhouse and I were in both the slalom and white water race with John MacLeod making the fourth team paddler for the river race and Nigel Morley fourth man for the slalom.

Familiarisation sessions took the form of paddling down the race course with Julian Shaw driving down the road alongside the river. He clocked us at over 20 miles per hour in places – which was probably the only feedback we received during the championships!

Just as in 1964, other teams set up training gates, and organised their own coaching at various points on the river. We began by scrabbling around an adjacent timber yard looking for bits of wood that we could use to make some gates of our own. The British Team had 'helpers', the management who worked tirelessly on our behalf – organising the campsite, attending meetings in generally looking after our welfare. However, we had no **coaches** because all our training leading up to the event had been individual, undirected and unsupervised. We liked it like that, or maybe it was that we knew nothing different. Despite the spate conditions, the three of us were totally confident in our ability to handle to river. Our confidence seemed to grow with the knowledge that the ladies event would be on the same course – and we could always handle any conditions that they could! Arrogance was an asset at such times!

Training sessions took the form of free practice on sections of the river, where each of us took turns in leading the others down the course and making breakouts in any available eddy. At times it was not possible to see the other two paddlers because the troughs between standing waves could be two metres deep and the peaks between the troughs could be ten metres apart. We frequently came off after 'brilliant' sessions. Our ability to feel in control in such conditions stemmed from hours of surfing at Abersoch on the Lleyn Peninsula where waves of eight to ten feet were not uncommon. The absence of slalom gates on the sea (for obvious reasons) meant we had style but lacked the precision of some of the other teams.

It came as quite a shock when Julian returned from a team managers' meeting and told us that complaints had been received about the British Team practising in conditions that 'ladies from the other teams' believed to be dangerous. In our arrogance, we thought it was probably many of the men as well on those teams! A decision had been made that nobody would be allowed on the course unless the river level dropped significantly. Furthermore, if the level did not drop by a full metre on the marker gauge at the end of the course, the championships as a whole would be moved to an adjacent river valley – the Möll. Obviously, this was seen as far more serious and dangerous by the organisers than we believed to be the case.

The river level did drop by just over a metre and the event went ahead. As a team, and as individuals, we performed well, but penalties reflected our lack of precision and positions of 13th,17th and 21st were probably fair results from 47 competitors. We were disappointed to be well out of the medals for the slalom team event but looked forward eagerly to the river race and especially to the river race team event because the high river level gave an increased technical element and would enable us to demonstrate our expertise in this area.

* * * *

Jack Spuhler who had competed for Britain at the inaugural world championships in 1949 was one of the big three in the slalom committee of the International Canoe Federation and was on the organising committee for 1965. On the evening prior to the river race team event, he called the team together and told us that two British paddlers had gone missing on a 'grade five' section of the River Isel some fifty miles away. All rivers that have been successfully negotiated by canoe are graded from 'one' to 'six' with 'six' being given to a section of river that cannot be attempted without significant risk to life. This river, like the Leiser on which we were competing, was in full flood and the degree of difficulty increased accordingly. Unfortunately, the road did not follow the river and there were sections that were inaccessible except by canoe. A search had been called off at nightfall and Jack asked us if we would scratch from the race and paddle the river at first light to search for them. There was no alternative. They were British and we were the only ones with the expertise to paddle this river. We went to bed, did not sleep much, and were woken two hours before dawn so that we could drive to the Isel and start paddling at first light.

The two paddlers from Chalfont Park Canoe Club were top division paddlers whom we knew well. Apparently there had been some confusion in translation and, instead of starting **below** Huben as advised, they had driven **beyond** Huben and launched upstream of the town. The first section of rapids they encountered was half a kilometre of 'grade six' in normal conditions. This was now a river in full flood which meant the chances of survival in the event of a capsize were minimal. One paddler, Tim Riddeough capsized but by the time he had surfaced the current had carried him sideways where he was washed onto a rock close to the bank and survived. The other, Philip Sixsmith, was still missing. There was no question of us paddling the 'grade six' section and we launched immediately below it, paddling a river that, by then, had risen above the confines of its natural water course. In places it was one hundred metres wide and was flowing through the pine forest that lined the banks. We paddled about ten miles, looking in places where a body might have become trapped, but hoping all the time that he might be trapped on some newly created island in the river. We never found him. His body was recovered several days later almost at the Yugoslavian border.

For the second time, a death had prevented our competing in an international river race. 1965 remains the only world championship where there was no British Team in the river race team event and, following this incident, all subsequent trips by members of the BCU and its clubs are expected to report to the team management if a major international is taking place nearby.

The rest of the season was fairly uneventful compared with our experiences during that summer. Once again, Dave Mitchell was national champion (which was no real surprise) and I finished in second place A greater source of rivalry had developed between paddlers from Chester and Manchester. Chester had John Woodhouse and Dave Mitchell but lacked a third paddler of their ability. Manchester had John MacLeod, who had broken into the top six during the year and who had been in Spittal as part of the whitewater racing team. In addition to myself, there was Ray Calverley who had become an international paddler at the age of 13. (He was already six feet tall by then!) The 'Manchester A Team' of Langford, Calverley and MacLeod was supreme in national events and beaten on only a handful of occasions during a five year period and **never** finished below second place. I believed at the time that Britain would possibly have had more medals in world championships if Manchester 'A' had been the national team during that period. However, this was impossible because team events usually preceded individual events, and were used by all paddlers as an additional practice opportunity. Dave Mitchell was the best individual paddler and it was felt that he **had** to be in the team in order to compete on equal terms. In reality, the selection committee had no information or technical expertise to justify leaving him out of the team. We attributed the success of 'Manchester A' to the hours of practice we had together. Even if Chester had been able to produce three paddlers to match the individual abilities of Ray, John and myself, our team was more than just three individuals. We knew each other's paddling style and were comfortable even when very close together on the course. The designated 'team gate', that all paddlers had to negotiate within fifteen seconds of each other, was superfluous because we were usually closer than that throughout the course. Dave Mitchell was a real individual. He trained on his own and was extremely competitive in his training. He did not share knowledge willingly – and certainly not with a Manchester 'A' paddler!

This Manchester / Chester rivalry prevented any meaningful co-operation in international team events that comprised a combination of Manchester and Chester paddlers. Such teams were simply three British paddlers on the course at the same time. At least, that was my opinion. Dave might disagree.

Maybe this was one of the big differences between Dave Mitchell and myself. He was determined to succeed, and did so by being totally single minded and focused on his own training. He was much more successful than anyone else in individual events. I had already started to look wider than my own performance. I was on committees at club and national level and took a greater interest in what others around me were doing – an essential aspect of team paddling. Dave's success as a five times British Champion was more likely **because** he took less interest in the performance of others.

* * * *

Understanding how others paddled and approached the course was essential to co-operating in team events. The logical extension of this is a need to understand how paddling can be improved. This is the basis of coaching, and I was interested. In 1964 in Merano, I had been a little annoyed, jealous, envious (or something like it) of the 'back up' available to other teams. In 1965, the organisation and administration of the team was good. We even had Jack Spuhler to keep an eye on us. What we did not have was coaching. More importantly, the paddlers on the team were individuals and did not want coaching. There was nothing against coaches, but what could the 'available' British coaches do for us that we could not do for ourselves?

One of the 'helpers' who had worked tirelessly for the team was Ian Pendleton. He moved from Edinburgh to Manchester in 1962 and joined Manchester Canoe Club. We trained together on the canal, but Ian was also interested in organisation. When I suggested in 1966 that we should have regular team training weekends, Ian was prepared to do the running around, sorting facilities and contacting other team paddlers. These were not 'coaching' weekends – because that idea had not been sold to paddlers. Instead, they were weekends that would bring team members together. A larger group meant more training gates could be erected. Organised timed runs were possible allowing comparisons to be made between the best and those 'on their way up'. There was a degree of motivation because competition was integral to the weekends. Obtaining accommodation and access to rivers and facilities was centralised. Frequently we had access to gymnasia. Finally, a team spirit was fostered – even though it produced a hierarchy or pecking order – which was not necessarily a good thing. Those higher up the hierarchy had a greater say in the activities provided. I can remember weekends at Chester which were made possible because Dave Mitchell's mother was in charge of catering at Chester College and contacted the college on our behalf. We had use of the canoe club and organised distance training as well as sessions on the rapids below Chester Weir.

One notable training weekend was at Llandyssul on the River Teifi. I organised teams who erected gates for the whole 880 yards of the course. That was the usual length for this slalom. It was ready in less than two hours. Then, after a short warm up, each paddler was expected to do fifteen runs down the course and carry their canoes back to the start after each run. This was **my** idea of endurance training and the paddlers agreed to do it! This means that each person paddled seven and a half miles but also carried their boat seven and a half miles from the finish back to the start. A couple of paddlers rebelled and only did twelve runs! We really were working in the dark on the physiology, but all kept going because they did not want to be the first to crack – or maybe it was that they did not know any better than I did. The weekends were successful because they were semi-official in that they were organised by 'a team paddler'. In addition, here were training weekends on rough water with gate sequences designed by people who were largely involved in the design of all the slalom courses for Division One. One weekend each month during the autumn and winter improved preparation for the start of the following season. The success of the weekends showed in the better results obtained by those in the 'squad', and training weekends became an acceptable part of preparation.

* * * *

The disruption to the international programme in 1965 that resulted in relocation of the world championships to Spittal meant that more consideration needed to be given to the venue for the 1967 championships. Many European countries were discouraged from staging the event because of the row over East Germany competing as the German Democratic Republic as well as the problems with visas that had occurred in Merano. Czechoslovakia offered to stage the event but the site at Lipno would not be ready for 1966 (the customary) 'rehearsal' event. Instead, the major international of the season would be staged at a 'new site' at Bourg St Maurice on the Isere in the French Alps. This was logical because the site had been highlighted as a probable venue for the 1969 championships.

Team selection took place after the Easter Grandtully event, and the 1966 team for Bourg St Maurice was selected to include John Woodhouse, Dave Mitchell and myself. Part of our international programme for that year was a slalom at Zwickau, East Germany, in May as well as the usual Monschau slalom that started our season. One of the new members on the team was Norman Jackson, from Warrington, who was selected for the river race at Bourg St. Maurice. Most of his training was done on the Bridgewater Canal but not on the section where I trained. John, Dave and myself had experienced the Leiser and Isel in the previous year and had some idea of 'big water'. Norman had not had that luxury!

When we arrived at Bourg St. Maurice and located the start and finish of the race, it seemed a good idea to familiarize ourselves with the race course – especially as we were entered for the slalom **and** the race. It was a long course (expected to be 45 minutes), and signs had been erected to show the entry and egress points. Having arranged to be collected at the finish, we set off. It was one of the more difficult race courses. A short section of Grade 3 was followed by a kilometre of Grade 5 rapids down to Aime. Then a further section of several kilometres of Grade 3 led to a steep-sided gorge of a few hundred metres where the river was forced between two rock walls about twelve metres apart. These walls were over twenty metres high, which meant the river could not be inspected before paddling it. The ladies course started immediately below the Aime rapid and stopped before the gorge. There was another grade five section immediately after the gorge leading on to the finish.

The river proved to be one of the toughest sections of river that any of us had paddled. Each of us capsized and rolled at least once on the section down to Aime. At least it could not get any worse than this because we had now reached the ladies start and quite sensibly, we believed, they had not been expected to paddle this section. The section down to the gorge was a heavy Grade 3 – big waves but no rocks. Then, as we approached the gorge, we were faced by a large rock wall on the right hand side. The direction of the river was not obvious at first and we paddled down into a large circular basin, about thirty or forty metres diameter, in which the water flowed anticlockwise. Then we saw it. The entrance to the gorge was a cleft in the rock wall about ten metres wide and at an angle of ninety degrees to the main flow of the river. The water surged into it. There was no chance to inspect the gorge from the bank because of the sheer walls on either side that fell vertically into the river. After discussion, we agreed that the gorge must be fairly straightforward because of the lack of access from the bank and we surfed across the main flow and entered the gorge. A river race would surely not be held here if safety were to be compromised!

In reality, the gorge was a mass of boils and eddies like giant mushrooms swirling against the undercut sides of the gorge. I certainly could not envisage swimming through here! After a couple of hundred metres the gorge opened out and after negotiating the final short section of Grade 5 we reached the finish bridge. Nobody spoke at first. Then the enormity of the situation dawned on us. We were extremely competent on the biggest water. This **was** our strength. Yet we were seriously concerned about this river race course. We had missed the 1964 race because of the death of the Austrian, Leitner in a practice session. We had missed the 1965 world championships team event because of another death. Now we were on another massive river that we were not equipped to handle. We were collected from the finish and driven back to the campsite.

The following day, the organisers of the event found out about our 'escapade' and were even more worried than we were. The dam-controlled River Isere for much of its length is used for the generation of hydro-electric power. We did not know this. In our ignorance we had checked the start and finish points but not the river levels. For the slalom, the flow would be maintained at eighteen cubic metres per second (18 cu/mecs) which provided quite a challenging course because of the steep gradient. For the river race it would be increased to 25cu/mecs. We had arrived early to practise for a few days – before the organisation committee. We had done our first descent at a massive 72 cu/mecs. No wonder the organisers were worried. A section of river that is Grade 5 at 18 cu/mecs is significantly harder and more dangerous with a increased volume of water. The narrow gorge is normally flat but, for us, the higher level brought us against the overhanging sections of rock and the increased volume created the surges and eddies that could have been disastrous. It was stressed that if anyone paddled the race course again above race level, they would be disqualified. We had no objections to that! Norman Jackson soon retired from river racing and continued successfully for several years in long distance racing.

The slalom and river race went without further mishap. Results were 'all right' but overshadowed by the earlier events.

* * * *

Back at home, there were important developments in the Division One slaloms in 1966. Although the significance was not fully realised, this was either the death knell for the complicated national ranking system that existed at that time, or it was the end of weir slaloms as a means of deciding national champions. Slalomists had two attempts at a course with the best one counting for the final result. Penalties of 10, 20 or 50 seconds were added for each gate incorrectly negotiated and 100 seconds for a gate omitted. Penalties mounted up, especially on the weir courses where lack of anticipation meant the boat was frequently pushed sideways by boils that appeared under it. More significantly, the short weir courses (80 – 120 secs), compared to the longer river courses (Grandtully was often 250 seconds), meant that penalties made up a greater proportion of the total result. The ranking points from each event were calculated by taking an average or mean of competitors' 'better' results and calling that '100%'. A paddler who was mid-table would have a 'ranking percentage' close to one hundred per cent. Let us assume the mean score at an event was 185 seconds. If a paddler had a time of 135 seconds with 50 penalties – total 185 secs, he would have a ranking percentage for that event of 100%. Winners of the more predictable long river courses had percentages of 75- 80% but the winner of a weir slalom often had a percentage of 50 or 60%. At the end of the year, the average of a paddler's best three results minus 15% – or his single best result – were used to determine the national champion. Dave Mitchell, John Woodhouse and I performed particularly well at the Division One event at Marsh Lock, Henley-on-Thames giving very low ranking percentages. At the end of 1966, the ranking list for the year shows Dave Mitchell, Ken Langford and John Woodhouse in the top three places, all with less than 40%. Fourth place was 51%. One event, a weir slalom, had completely disrupted the system to the extent that anyone not competing at Marsh Lock was unduly penalised in the end of year rankings. Remembering that several 'river paddlers' did not make the trip to Marsh Lock or Hambleden Weir (the other Division One Thames slalom), a groundswell of opinion grew against having top division slaloms on the Thames weirs. If the ranking system had changed early enough, Division One slaloms on weirs might possibly have continued. Instead, the complicated ranking system remained. The loss of Division One slaloms in the south of England was disastrous for kayak paddling to an extent that, by 1968, not one paddler in the top twenty was based south-east of a line running from Southampton to the Wash. Role models no longer existed in clubs in this part of Britain. Geoff Dinsdale, who had been in the bronze medal team at the 1963 World Championships, started to paddle canadian singles (C1) and was, arguably, the main *role model* for a major growth in C1 (and C2 paddling to a lesser extent) that began on the Thames in the late sixties as paddlers switched from double to single blade.

* * * *

The other significant change in 1966 was personal. I had been working a thirty-eight hour week in the Inland Revenue department of the Civil Service for just over five years. It suited me and fitted well with my training regime. Lunchtime sessions continued at the YMCA in Manchester. Evening training still consisted of distance sessions on the canal as well as the 'baths' sessions at Islington. Weekends were usually spent away on rough water – often at 'open' events in lower divisions. Division One paddlers were not welcomed with open arms at these events but were tolerated because of 'expertise' and help that we brought. Sometimes it was a willingness to judge but it my case it was a willingness to help with erection of the course and a degree of 'interference' in its design. I never knew whether I changed too much from the original design but the result was usually to the satisfaction of the paddlers. In exchange for our 'help', free practice time gave us more access to rough water at a time when anglers had a virtual stranglehold on access to salmon rivers. Although understandable, bearing in mind the high cost of rod licences, it was difficult to accept at the time. Relationships between anglers and canoeists are much better now than they were in the sixties!

One of the clerks in the office where I worked announced that he was leaving us and going, as a mature student, into teaching. Not for the first time, I asked myself why I spent my working week looking forward to the weekends. I had been teaching others whilst a scout leader, planning training sessions for the British slalom team and organising activities aimed at improving performance. Having investigated in more depth, I found that my GCE qualifications and the time spent working towards my banking examinations made me eligible to enrol on a teaching course as a mature student. I applied, and was accepted to study physical education and geography at Madeley College starting in September 1966.

* * * *

Life as a student was a massive change and required major adjustments. I had left school six years earlier, and had no experience of 'sixth form study'. The significant difference was that I now had far more 'spare time' than I had been used to – and did not really know how to make the best use of that time. It was to be a steep learning curve! My training as a physical education teacher complimented training as a slalomist. I was already one of the fittest students on the course, but had much to learn on the skills side – especially in the major games. I was one of the strongest but one of the least flexible. Working on these deficiencies was beneficial for my teacher training but also gave an added edge to my slalom training. I had sole use of the swimming pool for an hour each week practising eskimo rolling and gate work, and spent much time in the weights room. The interaction between myself and other students on the course was invaluable. Of forty students in my year, three quarters competed at county level and a third had international honours in their sport. I was one of a small number of students who had their own car on campus (I bought a 1955 Standard 8 for £35) and was able to get away on Wednesday games afternoons as well as weekends.

Madeley was one of the top ten physical education colleges in the country – referred to as 'Wing Colleges'. For me, its location one hour from Llangollen and Chester was just as important as its reputation. I needed a place to train during the week, and looked at various sites on the Trent before deciding on Stone – a ten minute drive from campus. The river was ideal because I could string four gates across at this point, and hang poles from the road bridge and from the pipe bridge fifteen metres downstream. In twenty minutes I had an eight gate course on moving water. During the three years from October 1966, many hours were spent on the Trent at Stone. There was enough light from the street lights on the road bridge to train in the evenings. Things were even better when the wooden broom handles were eventually replaced with white plumbing waste pipe that has become standard for training gates. It is easier to see the poles – even in poor light. The real bonus was using very thin 'fence wire' to support the gates – as was standard practice in Europe. The terylene bearers used for most slalom courses had the advantage of being re-usable but are highly visable and easily cut. Fence wire was not as noticeable and could be left strung across the river.

The quality of the water at Stone in the sixties was poor. Putting my hand in the water up to my wrist, it was impossible to see my finger nails! Nevertheless, my previous training had been on the Bridgewater Canal and the polluted rivers around Manchester – Bollin, Goyt, Etherow and Irwell. The Trent was no worse than these. It seemed completely acceptable for heavy industry to use rivers as open sewers. The improvement in water quality that has resulted from developments at Strongford sewage works south of Stoke on Trent in recent years has had a tremendous beneficial effect on the site for training. Of course the polluted water gave us one big advantage. Fish could not survive! The site was well established for slalom training before the river became clean enough for fish to breed. Consequently, anglers and paddlers do not compete for water time at Stone.

* * * *

The mix of athletes from different sports at Madeley College made me realise that, although more than competent as a slalomist, I was really ignorant of the principles of training. Other sports, especially athletics and swimming, were much more advanced in strength, speed and endurance training and peaking for events. I had been putting in the requisite hours but not making the best use of training time. In addition, performing under pressure and other motivational concepts were issues where many other sports were working on a different level. I was in a sport where **coaching** was primitive, at best, and often misguided. Looking back a the training session I had organised at Llandyssul earlier in 1966 made me wonder why people had actually followed my suggestions. But they had done! I needed to update myself and the opportunities to do so were all around me.

* * * *

Training went well at the end of 1966. By courtesy of the bailiff from Llangollen Angers we were even able to train on Llangollen Town – as long as we avoided fishermen. I won the first Division One event of 1967 on the River Lune and Grandtully selection followed at Easter. The 'Manchester A' Team of myself, John MacLeod and Ray Calverley were selected behind Dave Mitchell for the world championships at Lipno in Czechoslovakia. Ray Calverley was 'fourth man' meaning he only competed in the individual event. Dave, John and myself were in the team event that preceded the individual runs.

Lipno is a small town close to the border with Austria. The river is dam controlled, and the opportunity for practice time before the event was limited. Its location behind the Iron Curtain meant that few nations had been to the site prior to the world championships. The water was only released for demonstration of the course for ICF approval, and then for practice runs immediately before the championships. Without the benefit of video analysis, split times, or any quality feedback, we were already at a disadvantage when compared with the well oiled machine that was East German coaching. Furthermore, it was logical to assume that they, and the Czechs, had benefited from some earlier practice sessions. How else were the Czechs able to assess the suitability of the site for a slalom course? The gradient was steep, and the river bed consisted of massive boulders that made up the character of the river. (During breaks in the competition, when the water was turned off, we were able to watch a student from Prague University measuring how far his previously 'marked' boulders of varying sizes travelled downstream with the force of the water. I think he reached the obvious conclusion that smaller boulders travelled further than large ones!).

The team event was first. Too many mistakes on each run were expensive and we finished in fifth place. The East Germans took three golds and a silver in the four slalom team events. Still, it had been practice for the individual runs! Pauline Goodwin made her world championship debut but the lack of practice opportunity combined with non-existent bank support prevented her from performing well. In the individual events, the East German paddlers were exceptionally quick. Jurgen Bremer came first (with 30 penalties) Dave Mitchell with a slower cleaner run took the silver – justifying his inclusion in the team event, despite my feelings that the Manchester 'A' team was well placed to take a medal if Ray had replaced Dave in the team.

The 1967 World Championships in white water racing were held at Spindleruv Mlyn, a ski resort in the north of the country. The extremely short course (winning times less than eleven minutes for K1) was roughly the same time as the Dee Races that we were accustomed to at home. In the individual event Chris Skellern from Worcester replaced Ray Calverley as fourth man. Pauline Goodwin competed in the ladies individual event. Dave Mitchell finished fourteenth in K1 men. Dave, John MacLeod and myself were the three man team, finishing in fifth place – less than five seconds behind the bronze medal winners. This was the last time that the same British team paddlers competed in both slalom and white-water races at a world championship.

The combined total of paddlers for the slalom and white-water racing teams was **eight** including management. Things were about to become more complicated in future years.

* * * *

Until 1967, Britain only entered kayaks in world championships. Slalom courses on British rivers were often shallow and rocky and a single blade paddler would 'trip' on a blade that was longer and required greater depth beneath the boat. Technically, C1 and C2 boats were harder for the novice to keep in straight line and, therefore, slower and more difficult for the white water river touring – that many northern paddlers did outside the slalom season. As mentioned earlier, the lack of role models did not help. The exception was the Thames weirs. The water was deeper. Positioning of the boat was more important than straight line speed **and** Geoff Dinsdale was a role model. He had retired from kayak paddling after his 1963 success and took up C1 paddling – along with many other 'southern paddlers'. A group, consisting of Mike Hillyard, Mike Ramsay, Alan and Janet Harber, John Albert, Geoff Dinsdale and others formed a nucleus of canadian paddlers based on the Thames. Others, such as Jim Sibley from Windsor, soon joined. The growth of canadian paddling was given further impetus with the arrival of Joseph Sedivec and his wife, who had become world champion silver medallists in the mixed C2 class in 1965. Another Czech, Karel Knapp who was a C2 coach and lecturer at Prague University, also came to Britain and became involved in coaching. Things were not good in Czechoslovakia. It was the year before the Russian tanks invaded Prague. Karel eventually went to Germany to coach. His German was better than his English!

Away from the Thames, other paddlers in the top division were changing from kayaks into C1's and C2's. Often they were kayak paddlers, just outside the national team, who already had the slalom and rough water skills. The Witter brothers from Chester, Jenkinson and Slater from Leeds, and John Court and Jon Goodwin from Staffordshire were prominent names who fitted this pattern. Suddenly, there was an explosion of interest in canadian paddling! The national slalom committee arranged for C2 boats to be available to clubs who declared an interest in paddling them.

* * * *

Inevitably, the calls increased for canadian classes to be included in national teams.

The 'split' between weir paddlers and river paddlers had grown because of the geographical features of the country that had determined the type of water that people paddled and, to some extent, the type of boat used. It was nothing compared to the split between kayaks and canadians. It had taken more than ten years for British paddling to reach a level where it was respected across Europe. In the 1963 world championships, the East Germans had formally requested an extra one minute gap in the fixed start intervals for their paddlers because, in the draw of nations, they had been expected to follow Britain – and would catch them up! The request was denied and there were no problems, but it was a wake up call.

Arrogance is possibly too strong a word, but for many in the kayak team there was a definite feeling that many paddlers had switched to canadian classes, not out of a desire to paddle C1 or C2 but, because it was a soft option. Competition for national team places was more intense in kayaks. Furthermore, success was seen as directly related to the effort and time spent training. I was spending at least two hours a day training and most weekends. If a paddler had not been successful in kayaks, it was probably because they needed to train more! How was this going to be different just by having a different boat? For years we had competed against these paddlers and proved ourselves better than them in competition. Now, by changing classes, they were in the national team. Such thoughts existed but were seldom voiced and the two groups worked largely independent of each other. Off the water, there were no problems. In fact, when it came to gym work, running or other land training, several of the canadian paddlers were outstanding.

On the water, things were very different, skill levels for canadians were still at a developmental stage. Capsizes were common, and time was spent repairing damaged boats – either as a result of capsizes or, just as often, because the increased size of these craft meant that more rock damage occurred. At training weekends, much time was lost because a boat needed to be repaired. On the other hand damage to kayaks was occasional and minimal.

* * * *

At the end of 1967, Dave Mitchell retired and married. Much of his time was spent renovating a cottage outside Chester. He had been the most successful British paddler since Paul Farrant – with silver and bronze medals. I had benefited from the extra time and facilities that I enjoyed at Madeley College. I got to know John Court and Jon Goodwin who had started paddling C2. Jon Goodwin was working in the family confectionary firm and John Court was lecturing at North Staffordshire Polytechnic – later to become Staffordshire University. We seldom trained together because, as a student, I could do all my land training during the week and was able to spend most weekends on rough water gates. John Court became involved in squad training and, using his knowledge of exercise and training, we worked together on team training weekends. Once again, I finished second to Dave Mitchell in the end of year rankings.

* * * *

After the Easter slalom at Grandtully 1968, the selection committee included canadian paddlers in the team for the first time. John Court and Jon Goodwin as well as Robin and Rodney Witter from Chester were selected for the pre-world championships at Bourg St Maurice as well as several C1 paddlers from Chalfont Park. The team now consisted of all four classes K1 men, K1 ladies, C1 and C2. with a separate white water race team. The coaching team remained the same size!

After the usual Monschau trip earlier in the year, we arrived at Bourg St Maurice. The river was a respectable 18 cu/mecs, and flood waters from spring snow melt had changed the character of the river since 1966. It was a good course and an excellent venue for the world championships the following year. For the first time, decisions needed to be made about where we practised. The kayak team of previous years was used to working as a small self-contained group, even if each person was 'doing their own thing'. Now we had a large team and early sessions were frequently disrupted rescuing capsized canadian paddlers. Organisers only provided safety for the actual event. Individual nations sorted out their own safety during practice times. Inevitably, our kayak paddlers tried to find training times separate from the rest of the team. After the first few sessions, the problem eased. The Canadian paddlers adapted quickly to the conditions. In addition, the customary boat damage that seemed to happen more to that group meant that the water became less crowded! Although, at home, I had been very much involved in the organisation of training sessions, it was beyond my capabilities to find a solution here. However, John Court and the rest of the canadians sorted out their own organisation, and learned much of value in preparation for the world championships in 1969. The dominance of the kayaks meant that they set the training agenda and the standards expected from paddlers. There were no formal reprimands, and 'post-mortems' of individual performances were insignificant, but everyone was conscious of the need to justify their selection. The Selection Committee seldom attended international events. Their job ended with the selection process at Grandtully each Easter.

By 1968, I was in an unusual position, because of my 'unofficial' position on the Slalom Selection Committee. I was team captain, and attended meetings but did not vote, often leaving the room when voting concerning myself took place. I gave feedback on how classes performed in international events. The Selection Committee only had the final results, which were far from being the 'full picture'. I was also an elected member of the Slalom Executive Committee, involved in the design and erection of courses on which I subsequently competed. I played an active role on issues ranging from the siting of judging positions to the 'fairness' of courses appropriate to a particular competitive Division. I even acted as Chairman of the Jury at some Division Two events – where I was not taking part. Confidentiality, and impartiality, never seemed to be an issue – possibly because my place in the team had been almost guaranteed since 1964 as the 'number two' behind Dave Mitchell – and he had now retired!

* * * *

I was settled in my course at Madeley College, serving on the selection and executive committees of the Slalom Committee, and taking a major role in training weekends. Even so, I had more time than when I was employed as a civil servant. By the end of the year, I was national champion for the first and only time and the 'Manchester A' team were national team champions for the fifth consecutive year.

* * * *

It was obvious to Ray Calverley, John MacLeod and myself that, with the absence of Dave Mitchell, **we** as the Manchester A team would be the world championship team for Bourg St Maurice in 1969. There were no selection events. Decisions would be made by the Selection Committee at Grandtully once again. The only place to be filled was that of 'fourth man'. Keith Wickham was given the place. I was involved in the lively discussion that ensued concerning the selection of C1 and C2 paddlers. Some of us believed that only paddlers who could 'perform well' should be selected, and that any other course of action would dilute the minimal coaching that was available. Others believed that we needed to send full representation in order to 'develop the class'. Having said my piece, I left the selection meeting. Finally, the committee decided to send a team of thirteen that included four C1 paddlers, three from Chalfont Park and Graham Goldsmith from Brighton who did much of his training at Windsor. Robin and Rodney Witter from Chester were selected for the C2 event. Also included were three ladies so that a ladies team event was possible, which would allow them more time on the water. Ian Pendleton was appointed team manager.

Apart from the regular training weekends Ray, John and myself did regular 'team event' work, culminating in a full week at Grandtully where we were looked after by John Moffat, who owned the Grandtully Hotel and allowed us to camp in one of his fields free of charge. It was a conscious decision by us to work outside the rest of the national team and prepare for what we considered to be *our* best chance of a medal. We took a break from Grandtully and training to drive across to the River Awe and paddled from the dam below Cruachan Power Station, on Loch Awe, down to the sea. The Awe seemed to offer a large water catchment area, and we just had a hunch that there would be as much water as we were accustomed to at Grandtully. The map also showed a significant gradient which offered the possibility of good rapids. We were proved correct in all these facts and benefited from a good work-out on the river. This section of river would feature in selection events in 1973.

* * * *

The first international event of the year was Monschau – again. Britain had a double first place. I won the mens K1 and Pauline

Goodwin won the ladies event. In the team event (one run only), Ray, John and myself were paddling well and caught up with the team in front. We protested but could not have a re-run because the water had run out and the dam release had been turned off! Even so, German lager never tasted so good!

We paddled well and really were a team that knew each other's strengths and weaknesses. We understood the different ways we entered and exited upstream gates. We could anticipate each other's moves and take appropriate action to adjust without losing time. In fact, we had reached a point where our time in a team event equated to an average of our own times in the individual runs plus the eight seconds difference between first and third paddlers crossing the start line.

* * * *

As a warm up for the world championships, we had entered the Augsburg slalom because it was on the way and was two weeks before the main championships. Ian Pendleton had a long-wheel-based landrover, not because *he* needed one but, because he felt it would benefit the team. His altruism extended from giving his time as manager to putting money into the team (in the form of transport) at a time when paddlers were largely responsible for getting themselves to events. John Albert and Graham Goldsmith, with their respective girlfriends, joined Ian Pendleton and myself in London on the way to the cross channel ferry. We had collected boats from around the country, and were pulling a trailer loaded with twenty canoes. Several paddlers had filled their canoes with camping equipment and repair kits which added to the weight. In retrospect, the trailer was grossly overloaded but there was little we could do – short of leaving behind equipment that was essential for competing in the championships.

On the way to Dover, problems with 'heavy' steering became gradually worse, but this was attributed to the weight we were carrying and towing. Our route took us from Calais, across

Belgium to Germany and down the **autobahn** towards Augsburg. The steering problems became worse as Graham Goldsmith drove us towards Cologne. The trailer started to snake and, reaching the point of no return, pulled the landrover ever so slowly onto its side. The trailer snapped and crashed into the central reservation, while the landrover slid onto the hard shoulder of the autobahn. All this was achieved without disrupting the main flow of traffic and both lanes remained clear! There were no injuries – at least no physical ones – and we waited for assistance from the ADAC (the German AA). It took less than an hour for the vehicle to be lifted to its upright position, and for the trailer to be taken to a nearby garage. Damage to the landrover was superficial, and it was drivable, except that its upper part had been pushed out of line to the extent that the frame for the split windscreen was no longer square and there were gaps at the top left and bottom right corners of the frame where the windscreen no longer fitted properly. The two inch diameter tow ball (only available in the UK) had to be replaced with a slightly smaller metric 50mm ball – that rattled for the rest of the trip. The trailer emerged unscathed apart from a damaged mudguard and some damage to a few of the canoes, but these were repairable. Within three hours we were on the move again and travelling towards Augsburg. The garage suggested that Switzerland was the best place to get the vehicle repaired properly because the necessary parts to repair the steering would be available there. We decided that the priority was to get to Augsburg.

The course at Augsburg had been used for the 1957 world championships. It was constructed on the **eiskanal,** one of a series of canals that formed part of the hydro-electric system serving the town. Logs were fastened to the bottom of the ten metre wide canal creating waves and stoppers throughout the length of the course before it finally turned through ninety degrees and down a steep slope into the River Lech. At that time, the Olympic course had not been built. My abiding memories of the training site was forty or fifty training gates on a flat section of water flowing at about three metres per second. Within a hundred metres there were other similar courses laid out. A large club house had been built on the side of this canalised section of river. Training was unrestricted – until the map of the course was published. It was superb preparation for the world championships that were scheduled for two weeks later. Access problems to rivers in Germany did not exist. Coaching seemed to be taken for granted and was available for all ages and standard of paddler. Training at home could not compare to this. It was another world!

The Canadian classes benefited a great deal from the paddling opportunity but did not produce particularly good results. For them, experience on this type of water was invaluable. In the kayaks, I had a good run, finishing second and Ray Calverley, John Macleod and myself took gold in the team event. Problems of transport were temporarily put to one side.

* * * *

When we did leave Augsburg for Bourg St. Maurice, we travelled through Switzerland which was the European 'capital' for Landrover and stopped at a specialist dealer who looked at the steering. He informed us that part of the linkage had seized because of poor lubrication, and proceeded to strip down the steering system, replacing all 'faulty bits'. Ian was upset, because the vehicle had been regularly serviced – at least he had paid the bills for servicing – by the same garage in Manchester from whom he had bought the vehicle. Several members of the British Team had been very lucky, and they knew it. The garage completed repairs the same day and provided a letter for Ian to take to his garage describing the poor state of the vehicle, and offering to support him in any action he took against the company. Eventually, he was able to successfully use that letter back in England to claim compensation for all the damage that had occurred to vehicle and trailer in the 'accident'.

* * * *

It was a very sorry looking vehicle that arrived in Bourg St. Maurice to meet up with the rest of the team. Its upper section was twisted and it had rattled all the way from Augsburg because of the 'metric' towing hitch that had been fitted. Other team members were concerned about our welfare, at least until they saw the damaged boats. Luckily, most were repairable and there were sufficient spare boats to replace those that were too badly damaged.

The white water racing paddlers had arrived early and been ably managed by John Court in their practising on the river. The canadian paddlers had learned much from Augsburg and from their visit to **this** course the previous year. Knowing they had much to learn about the river, they erected gates downstream of the course and above the start of the river race course in the belief that if too much time was spent on the proper course 'before they were ready' it would be self defeating because they would be spending much time repairing boats after capsizes. However, time on the course increased as the event approached.

As kayaks with considerably more experience, Ray, John and I, along with Keith Wickham, spent more time training on our own trying out moves that we thought would be likely sequences for the championships. Our spare time was spent watching the French paddlers, partly because we did not really trust them but also because we knew that the Course Design Team would be watching paddlers, especially the French, to see what was possible and not possible on this course. All this gave us an excuse to train away from other paddlers in the team and, at the back of our minds, avoid having to spend too much time rescuing capsized canadian paddlers.

The event itself was a political nightmare. The East German Team withdrew because the French insisted in **calling** them 'East Germany. They wanted to be **Deutsche Democratische Republik (DDR)** or German Democratic Republic. The Polish Team also withdrew, possibly out of sympathy but probably because they were told to do so by their government. The Czechs stayed. After all, the Soviet Union had sent tanks into their capital city the year before and there was little love lost between the Czechs and East Germans who they saw as puppets of the USSR.

Despite the politics, we had friends in the east German Team. Christian Döring, who was one who spoke a little English, and whom we knew, arrived on the campsite very upset. His team were leaving on the orders of someone who probably had no understanding of the effort that paddlers had expended over two or more years just to be there. He was returning the Paul Farrant Trophy, that Juergen Bremer had won in Lipno, and wished us to give it to the ICF Slalom Committee. He could not face giving it to the French!

Each country was allocated training slots during the days leading up to the event. This was made more complicated by a decision to hold the slalom and the white water race at different water levels. Many teams had their slalom training sessions disrupted because the river was at the higher race level at their allotted slalom time. This was attributed to 'problems with the dam' but never seemed to affect French sessions! The major insult was when all the national teams were treated to a trip to Chamonix and a cable car ride up Mont Blanc. We returned to the site to find that the French had been training on the river all day during our absence! In my 'pigeon French' I complained to one of the French coaches, whom I knew reasonably well from previous events. His reply was – "The French Government have invested a lot of money in this event and they want results!" It was not worth continuing the discussion.

In the kayak team event the French had a brilliant run which no other country could match and Great Britain came second. We were really disappointed because our time was good enough but we had too many careless penalties. In the individual event Ray Calverley just missed out on the bronze and finished in fourth place. Keith Wickham, without the benefit of a team run, finished in eleventh place. In the ladies event, both Heather Goodman and Pauline Goodwin made the top ten. Despite their efforts, none of the C1 or C2 paddlers was able to break out of the bottom third.

I was not sure that increasing the size of the team from five in 1967 to thirteen in 1969 had done much to develop the Canadian classes! Time has now moved on and many things have changed. Selecting canadian paddlers who were not ready to perform competitively seemed to me, at that time, to detract from the realistic chances that the kayak paddlers had in that event, but it was really no different to selecting kayaks in the early 1950's who also had little chance of success. Without the commitment of those early kayak paddlers, the sport would not have progressed to its current level. Perhaps I have mellowed!

* * * *

Back at home, Ray Calverley continued his impressive form and became national champion, pushing me down to second place once more. John MacLeod and Keith Wickham finished third and fourth, justifying the team selection from the beginning of the year.

The East Germans, who had been denied the opportunity to compete in Bourg St Maurice, did enter the Llangollen Town International slalom in October – along with competitors from another dozen nations. I like to think their attendance was a 'thank you' for the way we received their enforced decision to withdraw from Bourg St Maurice. There was no jubilation because top teams had been forced to withdraw – just a shared feeling that the event had been devalued by the actions of the French. Llangollen International, the annual event, organised and run by the Witter brothers from Chester, was the highlight of the slalom year in Britain in the late sixties and early seventies, even though it had no significance in terms of ranking position or team qualification. But, it did raise the profile of the sport for the few years that it occurred. Teams were accommodated free of charge at the local youth hostel with the sponsors, Players cigarettes, picking up the bill. Sadly, the issue of sponsorship, paying expenses to visiting teams and feting the sponsors themselves, did not sit comfortably with a National Slalom Executive Committee that was fiercely amateur in its outlook. An event was taking place that was outside their control and concerns were expressed that 'a lot of money' was splashing about. There was no evidence of wrong doing or 'dodgy deals' but the committee was being asked to take too much 'on trust'. Few people on the Committee had the necessary business acumen to be involved in the organisation of an event on these lines, and they were not prepared be a part of it. Within a couple of years the event died. The issue of event sponsorship would arise again in subsequent years with the same negative outcomes. Meanwhile, the British team pushed on with its limited resources – relying on help and handouts from altruistic supporters like Ian Pendleton.

In the kayak team event John MacLeod, Ray Calverley and myself were beaten into second place by the East Germans. Their margin of victory was just over two seconds. Perhaps, if they had been competing in Bourg St. Maurice, our silver medal would have been bronze!

For me, it had been a good year with five medals in international events including a world championship team silver medal.

* * * *

The world championships in France coincided with my third and final year of teacher training. I had intended to continue into a fourth year to convert my Teacher's Certificate to a Bachelor of Education degree which was offered for the first time to students in my year. I had successfully completed the necessary 'bridging course' and needed to pass an entrance examination to move into the fourth year. Unfortunately, the date of the 'bridging' examination clashed with the international events in Augsburg and with the world championships. I was given permission to postpone sitting the examination until August and allowed to take it alongside those who failed at their first attempt. The course was filled by candidates from the June examination and no students were taken from the re-sits. I was now a qualified teacher without a teaching post. In retrospect, I would probably have taken the same decision again. The opportunity to be an international paddler would not always be available, and I could always take a degree at a later date. I applied for a post teaching physical education and geography at Otley, West Yorkshire, and started in January 1970. John MacLeod had started a one year 'post-graduate' certificate in physical education at Carnegie College, Leeds, in the September and I moved into student **digs** with him (and a group of others from his course) in Headingley.

I threw myself into the new job and developed basketball, outdoor activities (more rock climbing than canoeing), swimming and all the usual major games associated with being a physical education teacher. Initially, extra-curricular activities, lesson preparation and marking disrupted my training regime but gradually I was able to integrate training with my new life as a teacher. Time pressures were no different from when I worked in the Civil Service or the bank in Manchester. It was just a case of time management.

The first task was to find training opportunities to replace those I enjoyed at Madeley. Fortunately, John MacLeod had arrived in Leeds three months before me and it was fairly easy to fit in. I now had a training partner and was able to use all the facilities at Carnegie – often in return for helping out at events. One of the swimming lecturers had noticed me training with John in the gym and, assuming I was a student, asked me to help with a swimming gala. When I pointed out that I was just using the facilities and was not a 'bona-fide' student, he just said I might as well help because I was there! So I did. I was even able to join sessions such as pole vault coaching which John had enrolled on. My social life was based round the college, and I was even able to reserve late meals in the refectory after gym sessions. This was a time when student identification was not closely checked.

I was a Carnegie student in everything but name – and I did not need to attend any of the lectures!

Leeds Canoe Club was based at Headingley Rugby Club by the River Aire at Kirkstall, and had changing facilities under the main stand. Soon, we had short lengths of telegraph pole sunk vertically into the river bank and a course of twenty flat water gates on the river. Unlike Augsburg, the water was not moving and it was definitely not as clean. Several times each week we trained on the gates – assisted by the floodlights from the adjacent rugby pitch. Distance work was generally done at night on the canal that ran parallel to the river. We were less likely to paddle into obstacles and could cover greater distances that way. This was the first time I had trained regularly with other paddlers outside the monthly team training weekends. There was a social element to training nights! In addition, gate sessions could be more competitive and there was opportunity to learn from each other – where time was lost or gained in a sequence, or just comparisons of strength and endurance in the gymnasium or on the weights.

The River Aire, from its source in the Limestone of Malham Cove, was 'hard water' containing lime, which meant it was more difficult to get a lather when using soap to wash. Consequently, it was more suitable as the industrial water supply for Bradford, Bingley and Leeds and their associated woollen mills. The River Wharfe, ten miles to the north did not flow over limestone and could not be used to wash wool without producing large amounts of foam. There are no woollen mills on the Wharfe and it remains unpolluted and, as a result, an excellent fishing river. Access to the river was always difficult and disagreements with anglers were common. The one site where we had a good access agreement was Appletreewick. The landowner, although concerned that the site would become overused if he allowed too many people to use the site, did let us erect gates for training if we could remain fairly inconspicuous. It was similar to the 'understanding' that Dave Mitchell and I had obtained with the bailiff of Llangollen Anglers on the River Dee. Appletreewick was about twenty seven minutes and twelve seconds from Carnegie which gives some idea of our driving habits at the time!

Access to the River Aire was no problem. Industrial pollution had killed all the fish and the necessary vegetation for them to feed. From Bingley to Leeds we could paddle virtually anywhere on the river. Any non-canoeist who saw us paddling this polluted water would probably have thought us to be mentally deficient. We even erected more gates on the moving water under the Horsforth ring road a few miles above Headingley – and there was variety in the different colour of the water depending on what was being dyed in Bradford!

The training facilities available to us were certainly not brilliant, but they were better and more varied than most slalom paddlers had at their disposal. Apart from Manchester and Chester, Leeds was the strongest of the slalom clubs in the sixties and early seventies. Mark Markham, the club secretary, also served as Chairman of the National Slalom Committee in the late 1960's and the club attracted members from throughout West Yorkshire. I certainly had not come to some canoeing backwater. The grip that Manchester had on the slalom world was definitely loosening. In fact, as the biggest slalom club, Manchester was becoming complacent and surviving on its reputation. At least, that is how I saw it.

When Maurice Rothwell, Secretary of Manchester Canoe Club, had also been Chairman of the Slalom Committee, the majority of paddlers in the national team had joined the club – even if it was as their second club – in order to find what was happening at national level. I had begun to doubt the aims and objectives of the club soon after we, the 'Manchester A' team, returned with our world championships medal. A training site had been acquired on the River Goyt at Marple, south of the city centre. (This is still the club site for training and competition). An event was being held for the lower divisions and, as we had done at different sites throughout the sixties, we turned up to practise. Although it was a 'ranking' event for individual paddlers, there was an 'open' team event for paddlers from any division – a way of increasing club revenue. Rather than enter the team event, because we thought it would be unfair and seen as 'pot hunting', we (John, Ray and myself) offered to do a demonstration run and give club paddlers chance to see us perform. The event organisers accused us of trying to avoid paying for a team run and denied us the opportunity to do any form of demonstration run. We put our boats on the cars and left. The aspiring young paddlers never saw us on the water and, at a time when role models were seen as important in other sports, the club had lost an opportunity to promote itself. In comparison, two years earlier, the City of Chester had organised a civic ceremony to celebrate Dave Mitchell's silver medal from Lipno. Although I continued to compete under the club's name, I seldom became involved in its other activities from that time onwards. This incident left its mark.

* * * *

Back in Leeds, we became more closely acquainted with Mick Colgan who was very involved with the British Junior Slalom Team and had taken trips abroad to various international events. He was a teacher at St Bedes School in Bradford which had its own indoor swimming pool. John Macleod and I were given permission to train here with slalom gates suspended above the water. It was another addition to our training facilities.

* * * *

Within a couple of months of arriving in Leeds, I had bought a terraced house in Guiseley, five miles west of Leeds, and John MacLeod moved in with me. In addition, Dave Fawcett, one of the international paddlers in white water racing moved up from Manchester. The three of us shared accommodation – which was more like indoor camping but cheaper – with about eight canoes stacked on a rack outside the front door. Across the road was the local swimming pool.

* * * *

When I started at Madeley in 1966, I became friends with John Fazey who was one year ahead of me, and who became interested in paddling, joining Manchester Canoe Club while still a student. As a physical education student, he was also interested in training methods and often assisted me by acting as time keeper. By the end of 1969 he had finished teacher training and was working in Buxton. He had reached Division One and was ranked sixty-third. When canoe slalom was added to the list of disciplines for the Munich Olympics of 1972, I suggested he approach the Slalom Committee because there was always a shortage of help at events and training weekends. I would support him in his application. By the beginning of 1970, he had become National Team Trainer with Alan Harber (the Chalfont Park mixed C2 paddler). Together, they organised the training weekends – although anything related to paddling and paddling techniques was left to us as paddlers. Nigel Morley, who had been in the world championships in 1965 was appointed Olympic Training Squad and Team Manager. I was still a competitor and not ready to move into training at this point because I wished to go to the Olympics as a paddler.

Training weekends became more intense and there was a greater involvement with external agencies. One weekend was held at the Army Training School in Aldershot where pulse testing and work on recovery times was interspersed with trapeze sessions where we launched ourselves recklessly into space ten metres above the swimming pool. I am still not sure why!

Dave Mitchell was back. His wife for such a short time had contracted a serious illness and died. Throwing himself back into canoeing, he started intense training and even saw himself elected to the Slalom Executive Committee for 1970. This was a person who some years earlier had focused solely on his time in a boat and in training for his sport. He had a new lease of life – and canoe slalom had just been declared an Olympic sport. By the end of 1970, he had regained his place as national champion – for the seventh time.

* * * *

For the first time ever, I declared myself unavailable for the summer international events of 1970. Merano was to be the venue once again for the pre-world championships in readiness for the world championships the following year. Slaloms at Merano were always held earlier than other major competitions because the river was fed from glaciers and snowfields upstream. Good water levels could not be guaranteed much later than June. I had been teaching in Otley for just three months and felt unable to apply for three weeks leave, even if it was unpaid, during the main athletic and cricket term at the school. I had already been to Merano in 1964 and was familiar with the town. If I had been in the white water race, it would possibly have been beneficial because any additional practice was a chance to familiarise competitors with the course. It was less important for a slalomist because gate positions determine the course, and no significant advantage was to be gained by going to the site as a paddler. The team management **had** to be there. Administration, training facilities and accommodation needed to be right. I deliberated, and concluded that it would be better to show my commitment to my new teaching post.

* * * *

The school summer term ended at the end of July. In August, John MacLeod and myself competed in Landeck, Austria, where he took first place, and then we crossed into the German Democratic Republic (DDR) for an event at Thale in the Harz Mountains. It was a narrow river, comparable to Bala, and dam controlled in one of the main tourist areas of the country.

The thing that impressed me most was the course design. Rudi Landgraf from the DDR, whose wife had competed in the world championships in 1953, was one of the 'big three' in the International Slalom Committee (ICF) – as were Jack Spuhler from Great Britain and Werner Zimmerman (who had given the white water racing boat mould to us when we visited his home in 1964). Every single gate was a test in its own right and yet there were still many options in tackling the course. It was equally difficult for kayaks C1's and C2's despite the differing lengths and manoeuvrability of each class. This was how all courses should be – but weren't! Rudi Landgraf had designed it. Individual runs were good except that a **roll** on the gateline of the last gate put me out of medal contention. In the team event, we fell foul of East German 'efficiency'. All visiting teams had been allocated an interpreter for the team leaders meetings that were strictly observed – more so than in any other country. Our interpreter told us to be at the start at 'halb swei' which we took to mean half past two. It actually meant half *before* two, and we arrived at the start after our allotted time. After putting in a protest, we were allowed to start pending a decision being made. Our excellent run, or so we thought, did not count. We were disqualified before the result was posted. Our appeal had failed and we never found out our actual time! Once again, we had been found wanting not on the water but in the 'bank support' or, on this occasion, the lack of it.

* * * *

I did not regard non-availability for the pre-world championships as a major problem. I had performed reasonably well domestically and was still in the top three nationally despite the adjustments I had made in employment and in the move to Leeds. However, the Selection Committee did not share my view. After the Easter Grandtully event of 1971, I was dropped. Melvin Swallow from Chester was selected ahead of me and joined Dave Mitchell and John Macleod in the team of three for the world championships. I was selected as fourth paddler. Ray Calverley declared himself unavailable – as I had done the previous year. In his case, it was because he needed to take final examinations on his university course at Cambridge University. There was no selection event because there never had been. I had dropped off the Executive Committee in order to concentrate on my new job. Perhaps I had given the impression that retirement was on my mind – which it was not. John Fazey and Alan Harber, who had been added to the selection committee in 1970, never saw me paddle abroad during that year. I had been naïve. I had not done enough in front of the Selection Committee to merit selection.

I was still in the Olympic Training Squad and took part in all the training sessions on the 'new' Olympic course during the year. The site chosen for the Olympic slalom was Augsburg, a thirty minute journey from the main centre in Munich. The **eiskanal** had been redesigned since my medal winning performances of 1969, and a new section had been built based on a scale model constructed by a firm in Mannheim, near Frankfurt. These sessions were crucial to our training, because it was made clear that performance on **this** course would be the major factor for Olympic Team selection. The course was unique and unlike any other course on which we competed. The Germans were using smaller paddle blades about two thirds of the 'normal' size. This, combined with shorter paddle shafts enabled them to adopt the much higher stroke rate that they felt necessary. Other nations had their own adaptations but all were designed to cope with this new concept of a 'man made' artificial river course.

* * * *

I was given leave from my teaching post for the three week trip to the world championships in Merano. My absence was covered by a student from Liverpool who had just finished her degree course, and was due to start at the school in the September – teaching girls physical education. She obviously performed her duties well, and the lads I taught were less than pleased to have me back! She had impressed them and me. Eventually, I married her!

I finished in nineteenth place at Merano, third of the British paddlers. Melvin Swallow had justified his selection and was our best performer – in eleventh place. In the team event, the mens kayaks dropped to eighth place, which reflected the lack of working together as a team of three in training. In the C1 class, Graham Goldsmith was the best paddler in eighteenth place, the only paddler in either C1 or C2 to finish in the top half. A team of twenty paddlers had returned without a single medal and no paddler had made the top ten. The Olympic Games were only twelve months away.

It had become common knowledge that Jack Spuhler, the British representative, had been quite vociferous in voting against slalom becoming an Olympic sport prior to the vote being taken that led to its inclusion in Munich. His contention was that the sport was not ready. Certainly, it seemed that the British were not ready.

* * * *

Back in Yorkshire, training went well during the winter. I had won the Yorkshire Championships, which was a combined event in which points were earned for performance in both white water and slalom events on the same weekend.

At Merano, we had become friendly with Eric Evans from New Hampshire in the USA. He had expressed an interest in coming to England because we were able to train all year on moving water – because of the climate here. In Alpine Europe and the northern USA, skiing replaced canoeing in the winter while we switched to white water racing or paddled rivers in spate. Eric had been in the USA team for the last three world championships and it was good to have someone else, someone different, to train with us, even if the house was more crowded for the few weeks he stayed. His goal was to qualify for **his** Olympic Team for 1972. Working with him could only be beneficial for each of us.

* * * *

Late in the year I was invited to Australia for a six week coaching tour starting at the beginning of January 1972. This was a really good opportunity for warm weather training in the lead up to Olympic selection and I jumped at the chance – missing some of the training weekends being held in the UK. I was sponsored by Rothmans cigarettes who paid for the flight. All other expenses would be met by Australian paddlers and their families who would provide accommodation. I had been invited by John Egger who was the driving force behind Australian slalom canoeing and who was the first paddler from that country to take part in a world championship event. He finished fifty-seventh of seventy-four competitors in K1 at Merano – which is where I had met him and where we talked much about coaching.

In temperatures below freezing, I flew from Heathrow on January 4th calling at Damascus, Bahrain, and Singapore before landing in Perth where the temperature was 104°F (40°C). I stayed with Peter Dear and his wife, slalom enthusiasts who took a major role in organising the sport in Western Australia. The first few days were based at the Swan Canoe Club in Freemantle, where I was able to acclimatise and do gate work and some rolling practice in the tidal bay and get to know the club members. This was the main club in Perth, a city of just over a million people. Considering that Western Australia is two and a half times the size of Europe with a population, at that time, of less than two million people, I was working with the majority of the slalom paddlers in that state! I was able to work with a group of novice paddlers who were totally committed to improving their skills and finding out about slalom in the UK and Europe. This was a fledgling sport in Australia at that time. Then there was the hundred mile drive south to Bunbury and the dam controlled River Collie. The site was in a national park with very low rainfall, and reservoirs really were the life blood for the area. The river was only five metres wide with banks of solid rock where we could fry eggs in small depressions beside the river. Protection from the fierce rays of the sun was needed at all times. After instruction in putting up gates in a 'different' way – where **each** pole could be adjusted separately from the bank, we put up a fifteen gate course where paddlers had several attempts at it – with feedback from myself on the bank.

Paddling technique was basic. Few competitors could do the **bow rudders, high telemark turns or even simple draw strokes** that paddlers in England took for granted as basics for slalom paddling. The rate of progress was rapid and the process forced me to completely break down each skill to analyse **why** a technique was performed in a specific way. Why was a bow rudder better than a simple reverse stroke when entering a break out? It seemed simple but needed to be justified. These Australians were not content to simply imitate other paddlers. They wanted to know reasons, and I found it both very refreshing and beneficial. I started to look at my own technique even more closely to examine its efficiency.

After a week in Perth, I flew on to Melbourne. I would see the Western Australians again two weeks later when they had driven the two thousand miles across the Nullarbor Plain to Adelaide and on to the Australian championships in New South Wales.

* * * *

In Melbourne, I stayed with Roy Farrance and his wife, Jane who both taught physical education in city schools. Jane was Australian slalom champion and Roy, also a top paddler, was the focal point for slalom administration in the state of Victoria. Slalom was much more developed here than in Western Australia because it was less isolated, had more water available and more people involved. I spent a week, mainly on a section of the River Yarra, coaching paddlers from Melbourne and its surrounding area. Towards the end of the week, the contingent from Western Australia arrived in their modified coach, where extra space had been created by removing some of the forty seats so that more luggage could be carried. All the canoes were loaded on a giant roof rack that extended the length of the coach. The training concluded with a short slalom on the training gates that we had erected. Watching the technique, I was concerned about the number of paddlers who performed **high telemark** turns with the paddle shaft above the head while leaning backwards. This was common in Britain in the fifties and sixties and had coincided with a number of dislocated shoulders because of the poor 'leverage' position. I asked if many paddlers suffered from shoulder problems and was told that it happened 'quite frequently'! A remedial session was arranged, and hopefully was of some effect.

One day was spent on the Thomson River, east of Melbourne and in the next valley to the Yarra. It was in spate – which was the reason for making the two hour drive. We were joined by John Sumegi and his sister. John went on to compete and win Olympic medals in flat water events in the Olympic Games but on this occasion he was just another white water paddler improving his skills on a fast flowing river. Some paddlers were apprehensive about capsizing and this was having an adverse effect on their motivation to try new skills such as crossing from bank to bank in large standing waves. As the weather was hot and the water temperature was as warm as many swimming pools, we left the canoes on the bank and spent time *swimming* down the rapids. For the rest of the trip, the whole group was far more adventurous and, consequently, more effective from my point of view.

* * * *

After a week in Melbourne, it was time to leave and drive across 'the bottom right hand corner' of the country to Sydney. Even so it was six hundred miles, passing through the area made famous by Ned Kelly the highwayman. We arrived safely and I was 'passed on' to John Egger, whose family home sat on a hill overlooking Sydney Harbour and its distinctive bridge. Like many others in the area, the house had its own swimming pool that I was able to enjoy. After a tour of the city, Bondi Beach, Botany Bay and the waterfront at Manley, I was driven to Wollongong and introduced to the paddlers of Illawarra Canoe Club who trained on the warm waters that were the outflow from a large power station. One of the young paddlers, Gary Nelson, went on to compete at the next three world championships and I like to think I had some influence on his development. Paddling trips on the flat water of Botany Bay contrasted with being filmed by Australian Television as I surfed in a slalom canoe off Tamarama Beach, immediately south of Bondi, while the waves were breaking at four or five metres high. This place had been selected because the cliffs gave a good vantage point for filming even though the steep sloping beach caused the waves to crash from that height – unlike the neighbouring area where the more gentle slope made for longer runs towards the shore. Unfortunately, after fifteen minutes of forward and backward loops, I was washed onto the beach still wearing the seat and cockpit that had become separated from the rest of the kayak. The television people were happy with their fifteen minutes of film.

The final trip was to Newcastle, a wine growing area a hundred miles north of Sydney. Hunter Valley Canoe Club did some slalom but my role here was teaching surfing and boat control in waves rolling in and breaking at no more than two or feet high. I was able to show Eskimo rolling using the water for assistance. Two paddlers were able to hand-roll (without paddles) by the end of a one hour session. Once again, the enthusiasm of the paddlers was inspirational and I understood why John Egger had put the coaching tour together. He had contacted clubs from across the whole country and had arranged an itinerary to include as many as possible.

I did have a 'free' half day during the four weeks I had spent since my arrival in Perth. This was spent on a two hour sight-seeing flight in a small plane over Wollongong and the coastal area around Sydney. Then it was time to drive west through the spectacular Blue Mountains, past the majestic cliffs around Katoomba and on to the town of Orange. Finally we arrived at Wyangala Dam where the Australian Championships were to be held and where I would meet again many of those I had worked with in the previous weeks.

The nearest significant town was twenty miles away so everyone camped or stayed in caravans or trailers. The course was designed and half erected when I arrived. There were a few gates that were erected just to make up the required number, but which were no test to the paddlers. There was one sequence of three gates that was likely to affect the results more than any other area of the course. I was able to convince the organisers that there was more to course design than finding appropriate anchorages on each bank. After some amendments and adjustments, we had a good challenging course appropriate to the standard of paddler that would be competing. I had tried to position each gate or sequence of gates so that they would differentiate according to ability. I used the example that a maths test was not sufficiently **discriminatory** if it asked fifteen year old students to multiply five by three. Most students would answer correctly and we would still not have found the best mathematician! Slalom gates and gate sequences needed to meet this requirement of 'discrimination'.

'Free' practice was allowed – although the available water release from the dam limited its extent. I was on hand to offer coaching and 'walk' the course with any paddler who wished to do so. The event was a major success, being the first time that participants had attended in such numbers from across the country. I competed and left the event as Australian Open Champion for 1972!

After a few days back in Melbourne, I flew back to Heathrow where temperatures were substantially colder than I had enjoyed for the previous six weeks.

* * * *

It took a few days to adjust to training in the typical English winter, but I was motivated by the forthcoming selection for the Olympics. John MacLeod had been teaching in Headingley since

September 1970, but decided to take time out for a term to train full time from Easter. Having just had six weeks of warm weather training, I could not justify any further break from teaching. We each approached selection feeling well prepared but apprehensive. This was the big one!

* * * *

After the 1972 Easter Grandtully event which Dave Mitchell won, and where I finished third, the selection committee met. I began to have concerns when I was asked by one of the committee if I would travel as a coach if not selected to paddle. I simply said that I would consider that issue if the situation arose – not thinking for a second that it would! Each of us had been assured that the team would be selected on the basis of performance on the course at Augsburg. I had done well in competition there two years earlier, and felt that my more recent training sessions on the site had gone well. I had spent six weeks on warm weather training and been able to spend a lot of time in a boat in Australia. Then we heard that John Fazey, who was now one of the selectors and the only person regularly attending training sessions at home or at Augsburg, would **not** be at the meeting. Neither Nigel Morley, the newly appointed Olympic Team Manager, nor any of the other selectors had seen us paddle at Augsburg. How could they select a team? John Fazey had sent a note to the selectors stating his views but, in his absence, was not available to discuss issues that arose. The meeting seemed to take a long time and then the list was posted.

Dave Mitchell, John MacLeod and Ray Calverley were in Men's K1 with myself as 'non-travelling reserve'. In C1, Graham Goldsmith was omitted despite being the only canadian paddler in C1 or C2 to finish in the top half at the previous world championships. In C2 and Ladies, selection was as most people expected.

On reflection, I had probably 'shot myself in the foot' by not paddling in 1970 and then travelling to Australia in 1972. At that time, I did not think it made much difference since Ray Calverley had also missed a major summer event through examination commitments, and that was for a world championship! Nobody knew my level of commitment – and this, as I knew from my years on the Selection Committee, was an important factor in selecting teams, although not as important as perceived paddling ability. We had not reached the age of qualification through selection events.

Then, I was asked again! Did I wish to travel as a coach? I was just too disappointed, and declined. When I did travel as a coach – to Barcelona twenty years later – I could not understand why I had been named as a 'non-travelling' reserve for 1972. Other nations who sent reserves for their squads had had to go through a whole registration procedure for each athlete and official. I could not have been included as a last minute replacement!

I drove away from the selection event planning to spend my summer break away from canoeing and away from any Olympic involvement. In fact I spent two weeks on the Isle of Mull during the period of the Olympic Games. It was one of the first real 'holidays' I had taken for many years.

* * * *

The Olympic Games' canoe slalom events took place at the end of August. The internal organisation of the British Team could not match the sophistication of other countries, although paddlers praised the efforts of John Fazey for working against the odds to keep 'the show on the road'. Ray Calverley became ill and competed while running a temperature of 102°F. It was suggested that, if I had been available, I might have competed, but I do not think it would have been practical if I was expected to perform well.

All countries had closely scrutinised their Olympic representation and entries for the events were small in comparison with world championships, but these were the elite of world slalom canoeing. Across all four classes there were only one hundred boats

– the maximum allowed by the International Olympic Committee for canoe slalom events in these Games.

In the end, only Vic Brown, with a sixth place in Ladies K1, made the top half of the results. This could be viewed in two ways. Either we had competed at the highest level and performed at the highest level against top competitors, or we had sent more paddlers than deserved to go – based on the standard of competition. We had sent eleven boats and four of the eleven had finished in the bottom three in their class.

* * * *

The rest of the year was something of an anti-climax for me. Dave Mitchell finally retired from slalom, and Ray Calverley was the new British Champion. Pauline Goodwin in the Ladies K1 was champion for the first time. I had applied for a new teaching post and started as a lecturer at Stafford College of Further Education in September 1972.

It was a new start and I was working with a new age group. I even had considerable freedom over what I taught. At that time, physical education in further education was seen by many other lecturers as an opportunity for students to 'let off steam' so they would be more controllable in 'real lectures'. Officially, it was aimed at developing group interaction, personal and social skills, and general fitness levels. Performance skills were less important. How these very intangible aims were achieved was irrelevant. Apart from the five a side football, basketball and volleyball, I was able to develop outdoor activities, as I had done in Otley. Weekends to Snowdonia, day trips climbing and potholing in the Peak District, orienteering on Cannock Chase were new activities and new opportunities. In addition, it was quite acceptable to join in the activities with students – in the non contact sports. This served the purpose of maintaining my level of fitness as well as, hopefully, motivating students to a greater extent than being on the sidelines. At least, that was my excuse! But it worked.

At the college, I met George Clough, who lectured in the engineering department and who showed an interest in canoeing – because his son was keen to get involved. It was obvious that I canoed, because there was always a boat on the roof of my car so I could train at Stone on the way home. When I told him that I had made several fibreglass canoes from moulds and was quite proficient at repairing damaged boats, he became even more interested. Using his contacts (he had been at the college for many years), we located a room surplus to requirements and acquired a mould for a 'Soar Valley Special', a general purpose kayak that could also be used for slalom. Over the next few months twenty or thirty lecturers had joined our evening boat building sessions, and produced craft that they proudly took away for themselves and their offspring. We had sparked an interest in the sport.

By the end of the year, I had recovered from the Summer disappointments. My girlfriend, who had deputised so well during my trip to Merano in 1971, moved to Staffordshire to teach in Blythe Bridge and got 'digs' in Sandon near Stone. I had moved in with Paul and Annie Stringer who lived in a small cottage less than fifty yards from the slalom site in Stone. This, they rented from Mr Barratt-Green who also owned the land adjacent to the river. I knew them both well from my time at Madeley where they were also students. They had married, and Paul was teaching physical education at Alleynes School in Stone.

I was able to train on the river, as I had done three years earlier, and introduced Paul to slalom which meant I had a training partner as well. Annie, his wife taught domestic science and was an excellent cook, which meant I had really landed on my feet! I felt I ought to speak to Mr Barratt-Green about putting up gate wires on his land; I did not want Paul and Annie to be penalised because their lodger was wandering around on his land without permission! Soon I had erected wires across the river and made training gates that I could leave permanently in position. Although initially some wires and gates were vandalised and left floating in the river, their immediate replacement seemed to reduce the problem fairly quickly. It was like finding a building with one broken window. If left unattended, it would not be long before all windows had gone.

* * * *

John Fazey and Nigel Morley had retired after Munich, and it was necessary to prepare for the 1973 World Championships that were scheduled for Muotathal in Switzerland. The major point of discussion was the credibility of the Selection Committee onto which I was now re-elected. I was quite forceful in denouncing the way selection had occurred in 1972 and proposed that there should be specific events, identified in advance, that would be used for qualification. I felt that a situation had been reached where selection **was already** being made solely on competition results – by default. Few members of the committee had the expertise to analyse paddler performance other than by results, and I felt particularly strongly that they were unable to rule on a paddler's level of commitment, or his or her ability to be a good 'team member' who would have a positive effect on team spirit. Yet, in the absence of any **reasons** being given behind Olympic Team selection, comments and rumour was rife that such factors had been considered.

Although there was some initial opposition, it was agreed that selection events should be introduced to rank paddlers in the order that they qualified. The Selection Committee would only have the right to decide the 'cut-off' point, i.e. whether or not to send a full team for a particular class. Even so, there was concern that any paddler could have an off-day and miss selection – even if recognised as the best paddler who 'deserved' to travel.

A compromise was accepted. A separate event was arranged for the River Awe near Oban, in Scotland which would take place after the Grandtully slalom. This was the river that John MacLeod, Ray Calverley and I had paddled in 1969 while training at Grandtully. Water level was guaranteed because the Scottish hydro-electric board operated the dam half a mile above the start.

A moderate water release was available on the Saturday with a full release on Sunday. This was a long standing agreement with the salmon fishing fraternity who sold 'rod licences' (at several hundred pounds per day) on the basis of the quality and quantity of salmon in the river. All paddlers who finished in the top twenty in Men's K1 (with proportional selection of paddlers from the other smaller classes) would be invited to compete. Instead of the usual single practice run followed by two competition runs, of which the best one counted, all three runs would count, and there would be no practice run. After each run, the paddler in first place qualified, and did not paddle in subsequent runs. Similarly, for the second and third runs, after which three paddlers were ranked for selection. The fourth place was allocated to the paddler with the best average score, who had not already qualified. In this way, each person had *three* attempts to qualify – which was more than anyone had in a world championship. Performance on the day was important and needed to be recognised.

After the Grandtully event, paddlers made the trip across to the Awe. The course was to be erected by the paddlers. Members of the Selection and Executive committees acted as judges. I had designed a course which was shown to everyone in advance so that, if anyone objected, it could be changed. I had had the advantage of seeing the river with the correct water release, even if it was four years earlier. We would be erecting it with the 'tap' turned off. The course was accepted as fair and no changes were requested. Nobody had practised the course in advance because no slalom had previously been held here. In fact, few people had seen the river at competition level. On the day of competition, gates were adjusted to the correct height, and opportunity was given for inspection from the bank for an hour, but each person's first run down the course was a competitive run. Once again, John MacLeod, Ray Calverley and myself qualified. Mike Thomas from Manchester took the fourth place. Alan Edge finished in fifth place and missed selection. In the other classes, 'cut-off' points were decided, and the final team included two C1, three ladies K1 and three C2 crews.

I had been re-elected to the Selection Committee and been instrumental in producing a selection policy. In addition, I had designed the course. I suppose I could have been accused of having a conflict of interest but the issue never arose. After all, I had designed, erected or had a major part in most of the First Division slalom courses in the previous six or seven years. Anyone could have objected, and probably would have done if it seemed that a course was biased in favour of a particular group or class. Now I was back on the Selection Committee, selecting a team that would include myself! There had not been a problem in 1967 or 1969 when my place was almost guaranteed because of my ranking. Now, in 1973, it was even easier. The selection was being made on a 'mathematical' formula and there was never any doubt that a full men's K1 team would be sent. Although I was involved in the discussion about 'cut-off' points for the other divisions (because as team coach I could comment on paddling standards in relation to those in Europe – which several of the Selection Committee members were unable to do), I was not able to **vote** on the matter, but I was appointed once again as Team Coach with Stuart Fraser as Team Manager. Stuart was a member of Chalfont Park Canoe Club but had stopped paddling. His involvement in the sport in recent years had been as a sport photographer. Indeed, he had won a 'gold medal' in the World Press Photographic Competition in 1967 with an action shot of canoeing.

The majority of paddlers left this first selection event with positive feelings. All decisions were transparent and 'personalities' were finally excluded from selection. If this was to continue in future years the event just had to be a success. It was!

* * * *

In October of 1972, I had made contact with Stafford Newsletter, and discussed with the editor, Dave McLean, my ideas of starting a canoe club in the area. The article appeared on 6th October. The nearest slalom clubs were Chester, Manchester, and the Midland Canoe Club in Derby. All were an hour's drive from Stafford. There was already plenty of 'non-competitive' canoeing in the area. Staffordshire school children benefited from paddling opportunities in its residential centres and youth clubs. As the 'new kid on the block', I certainly did not wish to conflict with these centres, and decided very early that any club that I started would be for slalom and whitewater racing, and would provide a **progression** for those who had been introduced to the sport through education and youth services.

After Grandtully, 1973, I discussed with Jon and Pauline Goodwin the formation of a club on the lines discussed with Dave McLean a few months earlier. Both lived a short drive from Stone. Pauline had been selected in Ladies K1 for Muothatal, and Jon was in the C1 Whitewater Racing Team for the same event. His C2 partner, John Court had teamed up with Willy Reichenstein, a sprint C1 paddler who was teaching in Penkridge. They had decided to seek Olympic selection for sprint C2 at Montreal in 1976. George Clough, despite not being able to swim, was keen to be involved in a club in some capacity. We arranged a meeting in April 1973 at the Dog and Doublet Inn at Sandon, because it was half way between Stafford and Stone and had a room that we could 'take over' for the evening – without having to pay! Fourteen people attended, including another Division One paddler, Richard Baker, who came up from Lichfield, and Phil Baskerville, who was an active Senior Instructor working in the area with Staffordshire Youth Service. I was appointed Chairman, with Pauline as Secretary and Jon as Treasurer. We then had to come up with a name. **Trent, Upper Trent, South Potteries** and others were rejected in favour of 'Stafford and Stone Canoe Club'. Club nights were held once each week with a committee meeting every month. We were up and running!

* * * *

Stone was the automatic training site for the club. I had used it for three years while at Madeley College, and it was the only place where the gradient provided a series of minor rapids extending far enough to have a training course that would be suitable for slalom. Its main advantage was in having easy access to the water, which was why the outdoor activity centres used it as their favourite launching site. The number of permanent training gates was increased as demand rose. The river was deep enough, and a pipe bridge, footbridge and road bridge provided good anchorages for gates and wires, while the street lights were our own personal floodlights! The poor fishing enabled us to paddle without any conflict with anglers, and soon there were training runs upstream and downstream of the site. It took thirty minutes down to Burston footbridge and a further sixty to paddle back. The road bridge at Aston was closer – ten minutes downstream and twenty minutes back. Jon and Pauline made good use of the river for their river race training. The suitability of the site is reflected in Pauline's individual silver medal and team gold medal in the 1975 World Championships river race in the former Yugoslavia.

* * * *

Shortly after team selection, a problem arose because Stuart Fraser disagreed with some of the financial arrangements for the world championships. I never knew the details but understand it concerned **who** exercised financial control. As a result, he dropped out and, as the most experienced person available, I was asked to take on the role of Team Manager with Albert Woods as my assistant. Albert, had taken a large articulated lorry, containing the team boats, to the Olympic Games and understood more than most the importance of effective management. At Muothatal he was entered for the C1 event. I was Team Manager, Team Coach, driving a team mini-bus, and paddling in both the individual and team events. In addition, I was part of the committee that had selected the team!

79

* * * *

The team of fifteen paddlers that arrived in Muothatal was second in size only to the twenty slalomists who had competed in Merano. For that event, a case had been made for the maximum possible number to be sent to gain experience for the Olympic games in the following year. No such justification could be made for the size of the Muothatal team, but I had only been able to voice an opinion, and had not been able to vote.

The Muota is a natural river with no controlling dam. Merano had also lacked a dam to control the river level but, fed by snow melt from higher up the valley, sudden flash floods were less likely than at this event. We arrived to overcast skies that threatened rain which held off during training and for the river race that, for the first time, preceded the slalom. The slalom course was designed and erected, and then the rain started and continued unabated, changing the river completely. By the morning of practice runs, many of the eddies had washed out and several upstream gates were impossible. An emergency meeting of team managers was called and it was agreed that those managers who were also 'qualified' international judges would each re-site two or three gates in order to make the course navigable. I was Team Manager **and** in the build up to the Olympics had taken, and passed, my ICF judges examination. Although I was the **only** such manager who was also competing, this was an emergency and I was given the task of supervising the repositioning of the first two gates on the course. The only limitation imposed was that the 'character' of the original sequence should be maintained if possible. I was sole judge of that interpretation. Because of years of experience in putting up courses, the first two gates had been changed fairly quickly. I suspect some other managers could not even tie a basic knot or tension a wire. Inevitably, I worked my way down the course, giving help where needed. John MacLeod says he saw me still adjusting gates at the bottom end of the course, but I cannot remember. Once again the team managers met to agree that the changes made the course navigable, and safe. Then the competition began.

Most of the organisation and management of the team away from the course was taken over by Albert Woods. I already had enough to cope with because of my other roles. The competition was seriously disrupted by rising water throughout the event and very few paddlers managed to improve on their second runs. I finished in sixteenth place but Ray Calverley just missed the bronze medal by 0·4 seconds. In the team event we could only manage eighth place. Neither of the C1 paddlers were able to get out of the bottom third and the three C2 paddlers took three of the bottom four places. Our only claim to fame is that we were the largest team of non-medal winners. I was determined that this position would change!

* * * *

Having returned home, I was married in the August, with John MacLeod as my best man. Priorities were on setting up home in Stone. Canoeing took second place for a time.

* * * *

Muotathal, as an event, had lacked the atmosphere of previous world championships. This small Swiss village had organised things well, but the adverse weather conditions severely affected spectator numbers. The banks of the river and the spectator areas were quagmires and most people were glad to get away as soon as they could after the competition. An additional dampener was the dropping of slalom from the 1976 Montreal Olympic programme. Germany had spent in excess of £3 million developing the Augsburg course, setting a bench mark that Canada could not match. Even the last minute possibility of a site at Jonquiere (the eventual site of the 1979 championships) fell at the last hurdle despite intervention by the I.O.C. Also, many of the 'big names' in the sport, who had extended their paddling careers until the 1972 Olympics, had now retired. Britain was not the only country to see the exit of many from the sport at that time.

As a consequence, a new concept was introduced into the international season for 1974. The Europa Cup was between nations, and included both slalom and white water racing. Three slalom sites and three racing sites were chosen and each nation could enter a maximum of six competitors – with two individuals, named in advance, earning points for their country. It was a bold plan but too ambitious for the sport at that time. Countries such as Czechoslovakia were concerned about funding now that the sport was no longer Olympic. Only seventeen kayaks competed in all three slalom events. Nevertheless the programme was completed and became established on the international calendar.

* * * *

I found that Stafford College was a 'study centre' for the Open University. Since much of my lecturing was practical, I needed some academic challenge and decided to work towards converting my Teacher's Certificate into a degree. This had been 'on hold' since 1969 when I had given priority to competing at world championships. I was now ready. There was also a new incentive. I had spent ten years competing in Europe, and seen the advantages other countries enjoyed because of their team support structure and knew ours could be significantly improved. Coaching had been the canoeing equivalent of 'sitting next to Nellie' – a euphemism for learning from others by copying their behaviour without necessarily understanding why. Biomechanical analysis of technique was almost non-existent and coping with the pressure of competition was learnt solely through the experience of 'being there'. There was no financial support but we had two incomes now I was married. I enrolled to start in January. My foundation year consisted of a general grounding in social sciences and I looked forward to starting courses in the biological bases of behaviour and an introduction to psychology. This would allow me to develop greater expertise in human performance, physiology and psychology.

I trained much less that winter, spending time on my new teaching post and studying, and on training weekends for the national team. In truth, my focus had changed. Pauline, Jon and myself had started a new club, and I wanted to make it work. Previous experience of the complacency that I saw in the Manchester Club, and the way Mark Markham seemed to be holding Leeds together on his own, had shown me the dangers that awaited any new club. No club was going to be successful, unless the work load was shared within a competent and enthusiastic committee. The club needed to be more important than any **one** individual. I was, by far, the most experienced paddler, coach, manager in the sport and, rather than doing jobs myself, needed to pass on this expertise as a matter of urgency.

The first of the New Years Day races was held in 1974, with a 'Le Mans' type mass start from the Dog and Doublet at Sandon. Canoes were lined up on the canal towpath and we paddled several hundred yards towards Stone before dragging boats across the field, performing 'seal launches' from the river bank, and racing to the road bridge from which enthusiastic supporters launched buckets of water on anyone who seemed to finish dry. After changing, hot pies were available for all. This was our first social event and brought paddlers' families to see what this sport was all about.

We knew by then that we had the nucleus of a group that could organise an event at Stone. I had seen John Ferrie, the Chairman of Stone Town Council, about camping on Crown Meadow, which was an area of pasture by the river that it owned and leased to a farmer for cattle grazing. He discussed it with his committee, and approval was given – although I am not sure if they appreciated the number of paddlers who would be attracted to the event. At the Slalom Committee Annual General Meeting, our application to run a slalom at Stone, for Open and Novice categories, was accepted.

* * * *

Easter seemed to come quickly and team selection followed. The previous year's event on the River Awe had been well received and a mathematical formula was used again to select for the Europa Cup. Ray Calverley and I were in the team that qualified for the international at Lipno. Colin Ralph and Nicky Wain qualified and also took Europa Cup places. Vic Brown took a Europa Cup place in Ladies K1. Winter training had gone smoothly. Albert Woods had taken on the team manager role and I was once again the team coach.

The trip to Lipno was one of the most eventful I had experienced. Visas were required to cross the border into Czechoslovakia, which surprised us because, in the past, we had been able to travel directly to East Germany, obtaining the necessary documentation at the border – because we had official invitations. Now, the Czech embassy in London issued visas on production of passports. Unfortunately, Vic Brown was competing in Europe with the British Universities team and was unable to supply her passport. It was made clear that visas for Czechoslovakia could not be issued at the border, and, in an age before mobile phones, we were left with no option but to meet her at the Czech border with Austria, and then drive to the Czech embassy in Vienna. The border crossing point was about twenty miles from Lipno, but two hundred miles from Vienna!

I travelled from England with Albert Woods – in his car, and everyone met, as planned, at the border the day before practice runs. It was pointless arriving any earlier because the water was unlikely to be released before the event, especially as it had not been released prior to official practice – even for the 1967 World Championships. Furthermore, anyone travelling into the country, even on a tourist visa, was required to change the equivalent of fifteen pounds for each day spent in the country. This was partly to counteract a thriving black market in currency exchange, and because the Czech government needed as much foreign currency as it could get.

While the team camped at the border, Albert and I drove to Vienna with Vic Brown's passport – only to find the embassy closed. It would not open until 10.00 a.m. the following morning – which was the day of the official practice runs that started at 1.00.p.m. We returned to the embassy early the following morning and joined the beginning of the queue. Formalities were completed quickly and we left – James Bond style – towards the autobahn. Sharing the driving, we covered the two hundred miles back to the border in just under two hours, sixty miles of which were on single carriageway road. We met the rest of the team who were quite relaxed, because several other teams, including the Irish and their manager, Peter McIlwaine, were still waiting to cross. Driving to the front of the queue we crossed the border in convoy and reached the slalom site ten minutes before official demonstration runs. It was some time later that the paddlers were made aware of the full story. I needed to get myself sorted out and cope with the release of adrenalin that I had just experienced!

We walked the course as a team. Ray Calverley and I had competed at the 1967 World Championships at this site, but for the others it was a new experience. Amid intense discussion of the course, Ray walked separately from me and the team, and spent time planning his own approach to the course. When I finally approached him, he said "I cannot let you coach me if you are going to compete against me!" Initially, it was a shock. Ray, John MacLeod and myself had often discussed courses together, mainly for our **team** event runs. It was done to enable each of us to understand what the other two were going to do and avoid the unexpected. This was different. He was now one of the senior paddlers and needed his own space. I simply said, "O.K. I've just retired!"

The remark was spontaneous, but it just seemed to be the right time. I scratched from the competition and five minutes later, I was simply the **'team coach'**. I had started slalom in 1961 and it had taken up a significant part of my life since that time. Missing Olympic Selection in 1972 was hard, but **this** was one of the easiest decisions I had made. Looking back, I had never been able to avoid the 'distractions' of committees, course design, organising, making boats, new clubs, judging and a million other things that affected slalom. I did not have the single minded focus of Dave Mitchell. I was now able to focus on these 'distractions' without letting paddling get in the way!

* * * *

Performances at Lipno were good, considering the problems that we had encountered, but this was only the first of three slaloms that counted for Europa Cup points. The events at Bourg St Maurice and Augsburg would be included in the calculation of final placings. By the end of the year, Nicky Wain and Colin Ralph were thirteenth and fourteenth out of the seventeen who competed at all events, and Vic Brown a credible seventh.

* * * *

Back in England, George Clough had taken responsibility for making a set of competition gates and numbers and, with help from members, produced them in time for the first slalom to be run by Stafford and Stone Canoe Club. Numbers, well over a hundred, exceeded expectations, and tents covered a large part of Crown Meadow. The event was held in June to coincide with Stone Festival week, and attracted many spectators from the town. Although the club had not run events before, our paddlers knew what was required. There was no set standard to achieve, and nothing with which we could compare our performance. In some ways this was good because all aspects of the event had to be considered from scratch. Access to the river, the organisation of results, refreshments and dealing with spectators and car-parking were all new , and we did not wish to upset any of the 'locals'. The **new** Walton Bridge had not yet been built and there were potential traffic problems. I was still competitive and determined that everything would run smoothly. It did, and a standard had been set that the club still maintains in its event organisation.

It was never my intention to **run** a canoe club. I was fairly 'high profile' in canoe slalom and wished to keep a low profile in the club, if possible. Although I was Club Chairman, much of the work of day to day club management was done by other committee members. I voiced my opinions, as I always had done, and focused mainly on the direction the club took. It was established to promote slalom locally, and I would try to keep on that track. Club tours would 'support' slalom by giving opportunities to experience 'good' water, but slalom and the slalom site had to be the focus – or else why have a club? I did represent the club at the Slalom Committee AGMs where national policy was decided and where the club could keep abreast of changes that were planned. Having retired from competition, my real focus was in development of the sport at international level. I still remembered that the East Germans had asked for an extra minute start interval at Spittal in 1963, because they were following Britain, and it hurt.

* * * *

Regular team training weekends were held after the end of the 1974 season and it was time, once again, to decide on selection policy for world championships in Skopje in 1975. Dave Allen and Lindsey Williams had been the best British C2 for three years, but had still not been able to perform well at international level. All three of the C2's at Muotathal finished in the bottom four places. I raised the issue **again** at Selection Committee – as I had continued to do since 1969. I understood international grants were given to enhance performance in world championships, which were the pinnacle of the sport. Olympic Games were different – and funded differently. The 1969 grant was for kayaks but had been shared between **all** classes. There were demands from within the sport that funding for Junior Teams should also be funded from this 'international' grant. The result was that support was spread too thinly and no success would happen because we were competing against well resourced and well funded paddlers from other nations. That was my view. I proposed that only those paddlers who were **expected** to finish in the top half should go to the world championships. The rest should attend other internationals to gain experience and prove themselves.

The evidence was overwhelming, or else I had made a very strong case! It was agreed that the team would consist of men's kayak and 'anyone else' who the committee felt fitted this criteria. Selection events would be totally different now!

* * * *

At the end of 1974, the ICF made changes to the regulations that determined the dimensions of competition boats. Concave sections had not previously been allowed in the length of the kayak or in the cross section of the hull. This rule was relaxed and new designs quickly appeared. The German manufacturer, Lettmann, produced the **Perfekt**, which was described by some as a three metre boat with spikes on each end to lengthen it to the required four metres. It was sufficiently dangerous in the wrong hands to pass through a paddler's body without breaking any of his ribs! Very quickly, regulations were introduced to limit the minimum diameter of the ends of canoes and kayaks but, more importantly, 'uncontrolled' practice on the course was severely limited. In Britain there was an outcry. For years, paddlers had travelled to competitions and enjoyed unlimited practice, from dawn on the Saturday and Sunday mornings, until just before the start of competition when the course was closed and gates were adjusted for height. There had also been time for free practice at the end of each day. The safety of paddlers was at risk with this new design if 'free' unsupervised access was allowed to the course. Gradually, practice time, which was the **only** gate practice available to many paddlers in the lower divisions, was being eroded. An exodus of paddlers from the lower divisions of the sport started. Who was going to travel a couple of hundred miles to an event if time on the water was limited to fifteen minutes in a weekend?

In the Premier Division, this was less of a problem. These were exciting times. New designs meant paddlers were now able to sink the bow **and** the stern for the first time. More decisions were needed in the way paddlers approached sequences, because there were greater options available affecting optimum time down the course. Sadly, this was not understood by the 'average' paddler, many of whom thought it was making courses easier, because there was now less chance of hitting gates!

Before these rule changes, few paddlers in any division had 'clear runs' (i.e. without penalties). Those who did had usually secured a good final position. More importantly, paddlers could attribute poor results to the penalties they incurred. They would return home and practise until they could avoid touching poles. It was all very straightforward. Now, we saw many more paddlers going clear. Unfortunately, when they looked at the results, they were up to sixty seconds slower than the winner – and did not know where they had lost the time. Consequently, they had less understanding of where to focus their efforts to improve.

In truth, this analysis is not strictly correct, but there is a certain benefit in simple ignorance! A basic assumption (that reducing penalties would improve performance) had been destroyed. From this time onwards, anyone who wished to improve needed far greater skill in performance analysis, or they needed a coach!

In my coaching, I was able to dispense with the stop watch for many sessions – even with international paddlers. There were so many obvious changes that paddlers could make to their technique that were measurable in the reduced number of paddle strokes taken on a sequence. For example, the ability of the paddler to dip the ends beneath the poles without touching, resulted in a greater amount of time when the boat was travelling broadside down the course. Since it is much slower to move **broadside** down the course than with the stern following the bow, the less competent paddler was often sacrificing speed in order to secure a clear run. The less accomplished paddler, and his supporters, tended to equate clear runs with 'easy courses'. Obviously, this was not the case. A weapon in the armoury of a good course designer was to position gates in such a way that successful negotiation was achieved by **most** paddlers, but the better paddler was rewarded by reduction in the time the boat was travelling sideways!

* * * *

Streamlyte Mouldings had served the sport well with KW3's, KW7's and the later models of Scarab, Cheetah, and Scorpion that had been designed by John MacLeod. By 1975, Graham Mackereth of Pyranha Mouldings was working closely with National Team paddlers. His boats had been developed with Nicky Wain, Alan Edge and others testing the many modifications that Graham had made. Manufacturers had always worked closely with team paddlers, especially kayak paddlers, who benefited by having the boats on loan – to 'test' in competition. Graham travelled with the team to the 1975 World Championships. We now had something the East Germans did not have – our very own boat repairer, who was able to take the pressure off the paddlers and leave them to focus on the event.

* * * *

The 1975 World Championships took place at Skopje in the former Yugoslavia. The town had recovered from the earthquake that destroyed eighty per cent of it in 1963, but canoeing delivered its own 'earthquake' to the town. The slalom course, on the River Treska in the nearby village of Matka, was constructed using large metal **gabions** (metal crates filled with rocks) to restrict the width of the river, and create more challenging problems than were provided by the river in its natural state. The white water race had already taken place some miles away at Mavrovo and Great Britain Ladies had taken 2nd, 3rd 5th and 6th places on a narrow technical course in low water – perfectly suited to British paddlers. Pauline Goodwin, who took the silver medal, also paddled with Hilary Peacock and Peggy Mitchell to win the team gold. Morale of the slalomists was high as a result of the superb results achieved by the river racers.

A dampener was put on proceedings by a French boycott of the river race prize giving, because they had been disqualified in one of the team events for 'jumping the start'. Normally one boat is held by the starter on the start line, and the other two are upstream of him. When the starter signals 'Go!', the boat on the start must be first to cross the line. Unfortunately, one of the other boats crossed the line first – which is a disqualifiable offence. Unlike 1969, where they had successfully contrived to exclude the East German and Polish teams, events worked against them on this occasion. The International Canoe Federation, had to take strong action because one of the Yugoslavian politicians, who was at the prize giving, had been 'snubbed' by the French action. The ICF Jury disqualified the whole French team, including the slalom team which had not yet competed, from the competition and withheld all the medals from the French river race paddlers who had not attended the prize giving. Inevitably, the French slalomists protested because they had not been involved in the protest. On appeal, the French slalomists would be allowed to compete, but only if their whitewater racing team served a ban on all international competition until *after* the next world championships in 1977. The French found this unacceptable, and their slalomists did not compete at Skopje.

The British team consisted of four kayak paddlers, and Martyn Hedges in canadian singles. Peggy Mitchell was allowed to compete because she had been in the USA slalom team since 1969, had married Dave Mitchell, and was already selected for the whitewater race. The team of six paddlers was the smallest since 1967, and included five newcomers. Only Ray Calverley remained from 1973. The selection policy had been strictly observed. I was team coach and Albert Woods was team manager. Now it was time to deliver.

All the kayaks finished in the top half. Nicky Wain and Alan Edge took seventh and eighth places. For the first time, we had two paddlers in the top ten! Martin Hedges justified his place by finishing just inside the top half. Peggy, with less time training on the slalom course and recovering from her gold medal performance in river race, finished in the bottom third. A message had been sent to British paddlers that being the best in Britain in any class was no longer sufficient to earn world championship selection.

By the end of the year, Nicky Wain was the new National Champion in Mens K1.

* * * *

At the end of 1975, John Fazey resigned from his role as National Competition Coach, a job he had done since finishing with the Olympic Squad. After discussion with Oliver Cock, the National Coach who had guided Paul Farrant to world championship success, I took over the post. The aim was to produce some criteria that met the needs of both slalom and sprint, and constituted a 'competitive coach award'. Oliver had put together the structure for Senior Instructors and Coaches in the non-competitive aspects of canoeing. It worked well and had its focus on safety of the paddler, but this was different.

At the same time, Ray Calverley, who had retired after Skopje, took on the role of National Team Coach for slalom. Ray had been in international competition since 1967 and had two fourth places in world championships, as well as the team silver from Bourg St. Maurice. He had been British Champion four times and was perfectly able to take my place.

I tried to formulate a scheme for competition coaches but was unable to separate the 'qualification' from the 'job'. In other words, I was trying to certificate coaches and give them a piece of paper to that effect. In reality, a good competitive coach was someone who could produce results and raise performance levels. He had to be much more than a 'supervisor' of paddlers. As very few people were working with performers, any qualification would have been, at best, theoretical, and, at worst, irrelevant. I felt that what was needed was **additional** support for people already in competitive coaching. I could see, at that time, that having a **competitive** coaching award might lead to labelling of coaches as 'qualified' or 'unqualified', irrespective of their ability to raise performance. Some of those who had proved themselves best able to enhance performance had experience but no qualification. The theory of a competition coaching structure was sound, but the sport was not yet ready for it. After twelve months, I also resigned! It was sufficient to have coaches with qualifications in 'people management' and safety. The Senior Instructor Award met that need. Competitive coaches would be judged by their success. On reflection, I was the wrong person for the job. There **was** a need for slalom coaches at development and novice level, but not at the level where I was involved. It is very different now, but thirty years ago most paddlers were self taught and not ready for someone to wave a piece of paper at them saying "I am a coach!" Coaches were respected because of their experience and achievements, although I am not sure how a person was expected to get the necessary experience. It was hard for anyone else to 'break into' a very small clique. Unfortunately, that was the situation.

The position of National Competition Coach had one bonus. It allowed me membership of the British Association of National Coaches. Martin Bosher, who had guided the ladies to their success in the 1975 World Championships river race was also a member. I was able to meet coaches from other sporting organisations and learn more of their structures and organisation.

* * * *

Ray Caverley, as National Team Coach, took responsibility for **all** paddlers. I was not the most popular person with the canadian classes and, in any case, preferred to be working with the kayaks. Nicky Wain and Alan Edge were established team paddlers in 1976,but there was a more powerful paddler than either of these. Albert Kerr, from Carlisle, who had qualified for the team for the first time, lacked competition experience but was able to use his strength to break into eddies using technique that was unique to him. Other paddlers needed to position the boat, and drive into eddies before performing a high telemark to turn for an upstream gate. Albert was able to recover boat position from seemingly impossible situations.

The first Europa Cup event of the year was at Muotathal, at a level more suitable for slalom than in 1973. Albert was having a particularly good run and had reached the half way point when spectators started whistling at him. This continued, and he pulled into the next eddy and stopped, thinking the **judge** had blown his whistle. All judges were expected to have a whistle that they could blow in the event of an obstacle or another boat blocking the course ahead. Ignoring a judges instruction meant disqualification. Albert did not realise that competitors from other teams had seen him incur a penalty on a gate. The judge had not seen the touch, and signalled the gate as clear. The whistles were for the judge not for the paddler. This was a hard lesson to learn. It would not happen again!

Moving on to Merano, the next event, we had decided to spread ourselves at intervals down the course to 'police' the event ourselves. Paddlers would only stop if a voice they recognised told them to do so. Splitting the course into sections was fairly new, but it was necessary and, for the first time, it was possible. Bigger teams meant more 'bank support'.

* * * *

By December of 1976, I had completed the necessary courses with the Open University and had converted my Teacher's Certificate into a Bachelor of Arts degree in Social Sciences. I had taken modules in the Biological Aspects of Behaviour and Introduction to Psychology, but I had done more than this. My appetite had been whetted for more knowledge about issues such as motivation and coping with the pressures of competition. Sports psychology was in its infancy in Britain

– certainly as far as canoeing was concerned. I seemed to rec-
ollect, as a P.E. student at Madeley, being told that there were
ninety three Professors of Sports Psychology in Cologne and
one hundred and twenty in Berlin while there were only **two**
in the whole of Britain – one of whom was Professor Thomason
at Loughborough. The figures may be approximate but we were
a long way behind other countries in Sports Science, and even
further behind when considering canoe slalom. By contrast,
it was a major area of study in the United States and I sought
out books by Craig Fisher, Albert Carron and others who were
studying performance of sportsmen and women. Social facilita-
tion, the concept of mental arousal and mental rehearsal and
attribution theory were part of a totally new world, and dealt
with aspects of performance that would have benefited me as
a paddler. Now I studied them avidly because they seemed to
contain 'secrets' about which paddlers in Britain were totally
unaware.

My next step was obvious. I enrolled on a Masters Degree at
Liverpool University. It was not possible to get a grant but I was
working full time and decided I could afford to do the degree
part time – with backing from my wife. I studied modules in
the psychology of participation and 'drop out', the psychological
aspects of motor skills and movement, as well as areas of com-
parative physical education and the history of physical education. I thought I ought to include these final modules because
they would be useful in my lecturing at the college, who would
then be more likely to support me in rearranging my timetable!
I picked up an extra evening class and, in return for the two
evenings I was now doing, was able to take two half days **in
lieu** to drive the seventy miles from Stafford to Liverpool each
week. On Tuesday mornings, I finished teaching at half past
twelve and could be in lectures in the university by two-o'clock.
On Fridays, lectures were over by twelve noon and I could get
back to college to teach at one thirty in the afternoon. I got to
know the motorway very well in those two years!

Finally, my dissertation was based on the last twenty four

In my first folding JS Mark IV. Prior to 1965, all kayaks used in world championships had to be 'folding' – usually a top deck of canvas and a hull of rubberised cloth with an ash frame. Typical 'lightweight' kayak was 10kg. *June 1961.*

Winning my only event in Division Three (held at Bevere Weir on the Severn near Worcester) and earning promotion to Division 2. *May 1962*

Shepperton Weir 'open' slalom with John Hall, Alan Marsden and myself, competing in the team event for Manchester CC. Gates are suspended over tongues of water created by opening selected sluices in the weir. *(1962)*

My first international event; held at Monschau, Germany. The water level was similar to many British slaloms, and it was only three hours' drive from the Dover/ Calais ferry. *(May 1963)*

High water at Shepperton causes the slalom to be cancelled. All the sluices are open providing more opportunities to play on the 'big stuff'. *(June 1964)*

Surfing at Abersoch (Porth Ceiriad). An excellent way to improve boat control. The waves were often bigger than anything we would see on a river and possibly gave us an advantage over many European paddlers. However, the absence of training gates – for obvious reasons – meant we lacked their precision.

GB slalom and White water racing team at the opening ceremony for the 1965 World Championships at Spittal

Heather Goodman, Lesley Calverley, John MacLeod, Dave Mitchell, John Woodhouse, Bill Crockett (manager), Jean Battersby, Nig Morley, Ken Langford

The author 'crossing' the Serpent's Tail at Llangollen. Health and safety was not an issue at that time. *(January 1967)*

The complete team for the 1967 World Championships in slalom and white water racing - photographed after selection at Easter Grandtully.

Ken Langford, Dave Mitchell, Pauline Goodwin, John MacLeod, Julian Shaw (Manager), Ian Pendleton, Brian Palmer, Chris Skellern, Ray Calverley (Asst Manager)

The author loading Ian Pendleton's landrover for another international trip – this time to Bourg St Maurice. *1968*

My individual run - Bourg St Maurice 1969 World Championships – too many mistakes.

The Olympic Course at Augsburg. A totally new concept in man-made slalom courses. *(August 1974)*

The mist rising on the best natural slalom course of them all; Bourg St Maurice, on the river Isere in the French Alps. *(1974)*. The winter snows changed the character of the river bed providing a new challenge each year.

The World Championship course at Spittal, *1977*. Spectators, ten deep, line the course.

Albert Kerr (still wearing his crash helmet) being congratulated after winning the Spittal *1977* World Championships by a ten second margin. Richard Fox is in the foreground.

Peter Keane (C1), Ken Langford and Richard Fox after Albert Kerr's win. *1977.*

Albert Kerr with the Paul Farrant trophy. Eighteen years after Farrant's Geneva success, the trophy was coming home. *1977.*

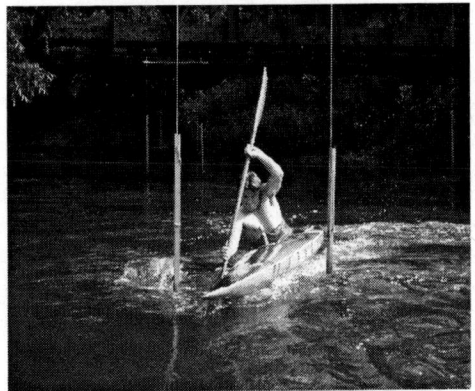

Paul Booth, an early member of the West Midlands Centre of Excellence on the river at Stone. Note the gates easily adjustable from the water by sliding the loops up or down the poles – essential for quality training.

Another winter coaching session with me at Stone. *c 1978*.

Coaching Paul McConkey at Stone, 1981. A lot of time was spent with the stop-watch on short courses.

West Midlands Centre of Excellence, cross country skiing in Trentham Gardens, Stoke on Trent. John Court (centre director) was brilliant in using photo opportunities like this to promote the Centre and raise sponsorship for training weekends

Richard Fox holding the Paul Farrant Trophy after his World Championship success in Bala, 1981. He went on to win the title a total of five times. He retired as the reigning world champion in 1993

hours before competition and focused on the psychological aspects covered in the course. The subject was "How not to blow it on the day!"

Then it was time to put it all into practice.

* * * *

My role at Stafford College, mainly as a provider of recreational physical activities for students, kept me busy, but was not really academically demanding, which was why I had enrolled with the Open University. However, it did prevent me attending international events as often as I would have liked. The college was absolutely brilliant in its support of my canoeing, and all leave of absence was given with full payment of my salary. In return, they would use my status in the sport to promote the College as a whole, and physical education courses in particular. I was conscious of the need to maintain the support of my colleagues who covered classes in my absence, and had to be an 'active' volunteer when new initiatives arose. Yet, I still did not think it appropriate to ask for too much time away on international canoeing trips.

* * * *

I had been actively running training events for the team and for the national squad. The Tryweryn was established as a competition and training site, although it was not until we had used this venue for a couple of years that Canolfan Tryweryn came into being, with support from the Welsh Sports Council. Initially, our usual plan was to turn up and speak to Miss Davies who, with her brother, ran a sheep farm near the top of the course. She was one of the real characters living in the valley. Her appearance, in a dirty raincoat and Wellingtons and a very unkempt appearance, belied the fact that she had regularly won prizes for her writing and literature at local Welsh *eisteddfods*. Each time we used the river, we paid nominal sums as 'access fees' to her but were unable to enter any formal arrangements. Bala was only a seventy five minute drive from Stone and easily reached for single days of training. Being quite narrow, gates could be erected very quickly and it became the top venue for team training. Pressure on the site increased when we lost the use of Bala Mill through poor control of people and cars at the Premier Division slalom at the beginning of the year. We had upset the local population. The organisation of the BCU Slalom Committee, and its affiliated clubs, was not yet able to handle access issues – even for competitors. I am loathe to think what would have happened if **spectators** had turned up to watch -en masse. After all, this was one of five or six **national** events where the best paddlers in the country were competing. Apparently, the last thing we could cope with was publicity!

* * * *

Access problems at Bala, combined with the four hour drive for paddlers from Yorkshire and the Thames areas, made less remote sites more attractive. Although Stone was central for most people, it did not have the volume of water to justify its use as a national training site. As a mid-week training venue., the site was ideal. Motorway links made it easy to travel as far as Grandtully, in Perthshire, in under five hours.

Matlock, on the Derbyshire Derwent was geographically much more central for most paddlers. The M1 motorway was twenty minutes away and even the Scottish paddlers could justify the travelling time for training weekends. The river was clean and there was adequate depth of water for the paddle blades of C1's. It was to one such weekend that Peter Keane brought a young kayak paddler who had been training with him in St. Albans, and who had made the British Junior Team the previous year. I was puzzled by the amount of his questioning and the intensity of his application to paddling. He seemed to be out to impress – possibly because he was not really part of the squad and needed to justify his presence. He succeeded on both counts. His name was Richard Fox.

* * * *

One of my **passions** in canoeing was course design. I had spent hours in designing courses that were more than simply 'guide gates' down a rapid. I had become concerned that some courses for lower division events were harder than necessary, and some sequences were more difficult than were seen on Premier courses. It was a disincentive to paddlers. I even suggested that paddlers on lower division courses might be more fairly tested if the minimum gate width was increased as means of rewarding fitness and speed. Nobody responded to my article. By 1977, I was writing articles suggesting that courses should take into account paddler ability to a far greater extent. I raised the issue with the Slalom Executive but do not think they really understood the issues! However, after much lobbying, the Team Management Group, of which I was a member, had been given authority to 'officially' approve courses that were to be used for team selection, and I arrived at Grandtully three days before the Easter event for that purpose. (By this time, I was once again the national team coach). Much of the course was already erected – which was unusual! I was appalled to see a sequence that required paddlers to **reverse** into an upstream eddy and continue to reverse upstream through a gate in the eddy. Furthermore, the justification for the sequence was that they (the Scots) had been practising it the previous week and had experienced no problems. I then understood why they had been so eager to get the course in position before I arrived! They wished to include a gate that **they** had tried out, but nobody else had. Arguments followed. I had pushed for control of slalom courses precisely because of the situation I now faced. Firstly, paddlers had trained throughout the winter in preparation for this event. This gate was, in my opinion, like working towards an examination only to find the syllabus had changed without anyone being told. It was grossly unfair. Secondly, courses in this 'new' Premier division had to be in line with international courses, because this was the logical next stage on which our top paddlers would compete.

I was able to overrule the event organisers, and the course was changed. I did not wish to enforce my own design because I had seen what happened abroad when one person was dominant in this area. Rudi Landgraf seemed to design so many courses in Czechoslovakia and East Germany that I felt I could predict with some accuracy where the gates would be positioned as soon as the bearer wires were in place. Other people's ideas were important. I restricted the changes on this course to significantly widening the reverse upstream gate, so that it would not become **the** gate that determined success on the course. I believed then, as I do now, that a good course should see an equal distribution of penalties throughout its length. According to White Water Magazine, some people thought the course was "brilliant". Others thought it was the worst course they had seen. I was in the second group!

There was some ill feeling when the event started – most of it unjustified. The Scottish group organising the event were very experienced. However, the course offered to competing paddlers is the yardstick by which paddlers judge the whole organisation. Prior to the start of competition, it is the **only** tangible information they have. This includes both the design **and** the standard of construction of that course. Doubts had already been raised in the minds of competitors – even if only at a subconscious level.

At the end of first runs, Richard Fox, who was a virtual 'unknown' to most of the paddlers, was given a time faster than anyone else, and would have been in the lead without a couple of penalties. Complaints and mutterings were heard about poor timing. However, when his second run time was seen to be only two seconds slower, people began to take notice. He eventually finished third behind Nicky Wain and the winner, Albert Kerr. It was Albert's first win in the top division, and he was selected, along with Nicky Wain, for the Spittal world championship team. The top six were invited to compete at Muothatal and fight for the final two places. Martyn Peters, the reigning British Champion just missed out, even though he later won the British Open event at Bala in June of that year. There were no arguments and no complaints. Richard Fox was selected for the World Championship! The policy had been decided in advance and Martyn had not 'come good' when it mattered. Julia Harling was so far ahead of Sue Small and Liz Sharman that she alone was selected. Martyn Hedges and Peter Keane were selected in C1, a long way ahead of the rest. The canadian doubles were still unable to show enough ability to be selected. Even in the following event at Bala Mill, many of them missed the upstream gate above the main fall, and then complained that the sequence was too difficult. I considered that move to be 'international standard' and that they were not! Apart from the C2's, penalties had been fairly evenly distributed throughout the length of the course. The C2's might argue that their boats were that bit longer!

* * * *

Muotathal was used as a warm up event, and for selection of final places for the world championships. Albert Kerr won, and Britain took second, fourth and fifth places. Alan Edge and Richard Fox joined Albert and Nicky in the Mens K1. Peter Keane won the C1.

Martyn Hedges, not to be outdone, won the C1 event at Merano!

The standard of paddling had improved significantly since the decision had been taken in 1975 to **only** send paddlers to world championships who could perform at world championships standard! The canadian single paddlers had responded magnificently. In all sports, the importance of successful 'role' models had been demonstrated many times. We now had two more who would, hopefully, inspire the rest of the canadians.

* * * *

It was my third time in Spittal for a world championships event. I had been a spectator in 1963, a competitor in 1965, and now I was here as coach. The river had changed because of landslides in this narrow gorge through which the Leiser forced its way. The changes were not important because boat design had also changed. Graham Mackereth was still working closely with paddlers, and able to modify boats to suit the specific needs of team paddlers for this event. Albert Kerr, on his arrival in Spittal, decided that there was insufficient volume in his boat. He phoned Graham, who had stayed behind in Warrington. A new boat was made and taken out of the mould while it was still 'green' (which meant it had not fully cured and could be 'stretched'). An additional strip was inserted between the deck and hull to increase its volume. The modified boat was taken by road to Austria in good time for the event. Although I was concerned about such late changes, I was certainly not going to make any comment to Albert. Confidence is such a vital factor at this level that if a paddler **believes** the modifications to be necessary, then they **are** necessary.

Paddlers were much stronger and fitter and the only significant factor concerned the siting of the thirty gates that would constitute the course. Albert Woods was team Manager and had taken care of all the administrative arrangements. He was able to make friends with managers from other teams and glean information from them. We had total confidence in his ability to keep us abreast of any developments. Consequently, I was able to concentrate solely on team training issues. Anything else we needed, Albert Woods would sort out!

* * * *

I had worked with the team and knew when they were feeling good. I knew when not to get too close, except in dealing with Albert Kerr. **Nobody** really knew what Albert thought. At one training weekend at Grandtully, I was working with the four kayaks who had been finally selected after Muotathal and suggested that he was not really putting much effort into each run. He just asked me how I knew. Everyone else was getting slower as they tired and was beginning to make mistakes. Albert seemed to be completing runs with monotonously consistent times, as good as anyone else. It was obvious! On his next run, he put in a time several seconds quicker – just to show me he could, and then reverted to his previous behaviour. I knew when he was *really* trying, and he *knew* that I knew. Neither of us needed to say anything more. He was not competing against anyone else. He was just 'sorting out' minor details in his paddling. Like Dave Mitchell, a few years earlier, he was happiest training alone and was not going to change just because other paddlers or coaches, were around! I told him that he could probably learn a lot from other paddlers by comparing his technique with theirs.

I must have made some impression on Albert because, after selection, he told me he was moving from Carlisle to Leeds because Alan Edge and Nicky Wain were there, and Nicky had been selected for the team. He said he was going to train *with* them. I told him I thought it was a great idea but not to train with other people. "Get them to train with you!" The important point was to build up total confidence that what *he* was doing was best for *him*. He needed to stick with his own training plans. Comparisons with others as they trained was not reliable because Albert would have no idea how much effort they were putting in. He, more than most, knew that to be the case and took the message on board!

* * * *

In Spittal, we were able to paddle on a large lake above the course. Albert usually wanted to paddle on his own so I drove him in one of the team buses. He paddled a long way from the shore, so nobody could contact him, and then returned – usually thirty or forty minutes later. There was no discussion. He commented that it was the nearest thing to home – training in total isolation.

Everyone else worked in groups because they liked the company of other people. Water sessions included setting gate sequences above and below the course – sharing with other nations who also erected training gates, but whose allocated training slots did not coincide with ours.

Once the main wires were put across the river, we had a further day to practise before the gates were positioned. I came up with my plan of where each gate would **probably** be sited. I was about seventy five per cent correct. (Other nations came up with their interpretations based on the position of the wires). This gave us chance to finish training with some full length runs to get used to the length of the course. Crossing the river, exiting upstream gates, and working against the river flow are much more difficult after three minutes of hard paddling. We needed to experience this, and plan strategies accordingly.

In the actual event, Peter Keane finished in a creditable twelfth place while Martyn Hedges realised that paddling both slalom and whitewater racing at the same event was no longer realistic. He should have already learnt this from Peggy Mitchell who was unable to impress in the slalom at Skopje after her performances in the river race. Julia Harling, as the only lady paddler, trained without adequate support and, unsurprisingly, was unable to perform anywhere close to her capability. I felt guilty, but it was difficult to include her in training with either the K1 men or the canadians. It was even more difficult to have gate sessions with Julia alone on the water, and me on the bank. A compromise of sorts was achieved by her paddling at the same time as other teams who shared our training slots. I could then do some 'one to one' coaching while other countries unwittingly acted as safety boat by just being there!

The first runs of the K1 Men saw Nicky Wain go well and take fourth place. He would have been in a medal position without a penalty on the last gate. Disappointing from my point of view was Albert, who had paddled steadily – as though he was still at Grandtully on a training run. It was usually fairly straightforward to talk to paddlers after their runs. Invariably, each of them had analysed their runs and knew what they needed to do next time. My role was to agree with them and support them. It was not appropriate to tell them that their analysis was wrong – at least not at that stage. Albert was different. He said nothing and, as usual, just shrugged his shoulders. Here was the most powerful paddler I had ever coached; someone who could pull the boat sideways more effectively than anyone else, but who had 'cruised' his first run. I just said something on the lines of – "Same pace again, but put more effort into each upstream gate, and sprint *flat out* between 22 and 23" – which were upstream gates on either side of the main current. My perception was that many paddlers seemed content to ferry glide between them, or were over cautious. The conversation was one sided and took less than thirty seconds. He had not asked for any advice so I left it at that and walked away.

Albert disappeared and turned up for his second run with only a couple of minutes to spare. I have no idea where he went but maybe, just maybe, he was looking at other paddlers on the critical sequence of gates 22 and 23.

The start interval between competitors was fixed. Each nation had drawn for start position which meant a gap of nine or ten minutes between each of our competitors. I had run down the course with each person but had only got back in time to see Albert breaking out for upstream gate 17. He was clear at that point, and a growing army of supporters were running down the bank with him. He crossed from Gate 22 to 23 with the boat broadside to the current, and looked as though he would be washed downstream – except for the power he then unleashed which took him across to the eddy. He took a couple of extra strokes to get through Gate 23. The final two upstream gates were safely negotiated with a couple more 'extra' strokes, and then it was a final sprint to the finish. I reached the finish line at the same time as he did. I calculated that he had lost four or five seconds on the cross between upstream gates 22 and 23, and from gate 23 to the finish.

The score board showed his time as 220·80 seconds, which made no sense to me because it was twelve seconds better than Norbert Sattler who led at the end of first runs and I had seen these four or five wasted seconds. Then the announcer said "no penalties". Albert was in the lead by over twelve seconds. It was not a nervous wait because everyone was in a state of shock, not knowing whether the timing had gone wrong. We did not dare to believe – until the last competitor had finished. Later, Alan Edge informed me that his abiding vision was of Siegbert Horn, the Olympic Champion of 1972 and reigning world champion, paddling up through Gate 28 with two gates still left, and looking up at the clock on the scoreboard as his running time passed the 220 seconds that Albert had posted.

Then the place erupted. Competitors wanted to congratulate Albert Kerr, the new world champion. Unfortunately, few people outside the British Team knew what he looked like, and there was a delay until he was located. I was able to climb onto the top of the timing hut at the finish, and watch events unfold beneath me. No-one looked up, and I was able to enjoy the moment by myself – almost as much as the letter that Albert sent to me a few weeks later. The Paul Farrant Trophy had actually come home and it felt absolutely great.

Alan Edge made mistakes on both runs. Nicky Wain finished in tenth place. Almost unnoticed was Richard Fox in twenty seventh place. He had trained separately from the other three kayaks for much of the build up to the championships. His time had not yet come.

* * * *

The Olympic Games in Montreal had not been successful for Great Britain. In fact the medal tally had gone down gradually from twenty four at Melbourne in 1956 to thirteen at Mexico (where altitude had been a problem for most European nations). Now, it had equalled that low point again. Dennis Howell, the Minister of Sport in the Labour Government of the day had established **SportsAid**, previously known as the Sports Aid Foundation. It was a charity designed to raise funds from the private sector of industry and commerce to help young people, aged eleven to eighteen, and people with disabilities to participate in sport. Seeing the Montreal results, he also established the idea of **Centres of Excellence for Sport**, requiring regional Sports Councils to grant aid sports groups who could work with athletes to raise the medal potential of the country. At the time, he said that these were to be the pinnacle of sport in each region, and had the specific function of raising standards of **elite** performers and getting international medals. Funds were distributed from Central Government for this purpose.

John Court, who always had an eye on such opportunities, discussed with me the possibility of applying on behalf of canoe slalom. It sounded good to me. An application was made to West Midlands Sports Council. At the same time, Mark Markham submitted an application to the Yorkshire and Humberside region, and Brian Horn (a lecturer at Edge Hill College in Ormskirk) submitted his application to the North West Sports Council in Manchester.

All three applications were successful and the process of recruitment began. Stafford and Stone Canoe Club was the obvious base for the Midlands, being ideally located one hour from Llangollen, Chester, and Matlock, which were much used training sites. The Jackfield Rapids, at Ironbridge on the Severn, were even closer. The 'new' site at Canolfan Tryweryn (Bala Whitewater Centre) was only an hour and a half away and was now a venue for international slalom as well as Premier events.

The highest ranked paddlers we recruited were Andy Sutherland (9th), Bill Berrisford (10th) and Paul McConkey (16th). Other Stafford and Stone paddlers were given invitations, and many joined – including Mike Berwick, Paul Booth, Alistair Baillie and Chris Edwards An application was also received from Liz Sharman who, although living in Bury St Edmunds, was considering coming to college in the area because Bury St Edmunds was not best suited for training on white water! We had had serious discussions at the Bala Mill event earlier in the year because she had progressed quickly from Novice to Division One (the top ladies Division) in one year, and was a little concerned about her ability to handle the **really** rough water at that site. She was less concerned about the volume of water, and more concerned about the technical nature of the site with its pronounced rocks and small eddies. It was an irrelevant discussion because by the end of 1977 she was ranked third in Britain and had been briefly considered for the world championships of that year.

After the world championships, Richard Fox had asked me to coach him – possibly on Albert Kerr's recommendation. I had agreed. on condition he was prepared to move to Staffordshire and put in "as much time as I was doing". The move north was not possible because he had lost a lot of time from his educational studies, and needed to complete his GCE 'A' levels before he could move anywhere. John Court had already said he might be able to get him some financial support. He was good at that! Meanwhile, Richard travelled to Stone at weekends, usually staying with Bill Berrisford. The offer of 'full' membership of the centre remained, but care was needed because the West Midlands Sports Council would not have been too pleased if a 'non-resident' was being funded from their limited resources. John Court and myself felt we could justify his membership (if it became necessary to do so) because he seemed to be a natural leader, playing a major role in decisions. His membership was of massive benefit to the Centre as a whole. The Centre of Excellence was well established. In addition to finance from the West Midlands Sports Council, John Court, had been able to obtain additional funding. A local Renault dealer lent us cars for training weekends. Training gates were made that could be taken to sessions on the Wye at Symonds Yat, the Clywedog at Llanidloes, the Tryweryn at Bala, and more local sites such as Matlock and Oakamoor. More importantly, coaching during the week was introduced for those who lived close enough to benefit from it.

* * * *

I was able to arrange my teaching to give 'breaks' during the day. I could get to Stone in fifteen minutes. Employment in Further Education was contracted at twenty hours contact 'time' each week with a further ten hours of 'departmental duty'. Any extra preparation, marking, or development work could be done away from the college – at home. The contact hours were fixed but the departmental duty time could be moved to create blocks of 'free time'. Working two evenings each week gave two half days that could also be used for coaching. I was able to spend a couple of hours during the day, three times each week to coach anyone who wanted to be coached!

* * * *

Since its establishment, the Centre of Excellence for Slalom Canoeing in Stone had developed into an 'organisation' that was better than anywhere else in the country. This was at a time when few people could get grants, sponsorship, or scholarships to train for their sport, and slalom canoeing was behind many sports in this regard. John Court dealt with the West Midlands Sports Council in Birmingham, and was able to obtain and administer the grant that would able us to pay for equipment, coaching expenses and transport costs. In addition, his knack of seeking out promotional opportunities, press coverage and sponsorship from Renault and other organisations, meant that I could concentrate solely on coaching. Later on, we had applications from Sue Garriock from Preston, and Jane Roderick from Formby, who enrolled on courses in the Art and Design Department at Stafford College – which made them eligible for the Centre of Excellence because they moved down and became residents in the area.

There was no payment for coaching, but I received travelling expenses which meant I could spend even more time with paddlers. In addition, I was employed by a very supportive college that allowed me to adjust my teaching hours not only for coaching but also to enable me to study for my Masters Degree in Liverpool.

The location of the Centre, based on Stafford and Stone Canoe Club, was mutually beneficial to both parties. The club had grown into one of the top organisers of slalom, and was running Premier Division Events and doing course erection for national and international events. I was still designing many courses and serving on Team Management and Section Committees at national level. The club was among the first to know of any new developments in the sport, and could contribute to any debate that affected the direction in which the sport was progressing. The status of the club kept rising because of the influx of members of the Centre of Excellence who became members because it gave them access to the training facilities and to an active group of canoeists enthusiastic about slalom. The club gained new **role models** overnight who would inspire paddlers and show them what was meant by **real training**. I had not forgotten the way I started at Islington Baths in Manchester with my 'role' models – and the way it shaped my own training. The amount, type and intensity of training that was adopted by the average club paddler increased because of the influence of the **Centre** paddlers. There was an acceptance and greater understanding of the benefits of training, and the trial and error approach that typified slalom training, became gradually more structured as its value became appreciated by all. If the paddlers were among the best in the country, their training would become the standard for the majority of paddlers – irrespective of ability.

Of course, membership of the Centre of Excellence was by **invitation** and it was important to avoid a 'them versus us' mentality. It could not be a clique and we tried to be completely open, ensuring that **everyone** who reached the right standard was invited to join – provided they met the residence criteria. The first problem arose when Bill Berrisford, who lived in Stone and who had been accepted as a kayak paddler, decided to switch to canadian singles. John Court and I decided that, as Bill's continued membership was not depriving anyone else of a place, he could remain a member until the end of the year because he had shown himself to be committed to slalom through his kayak ranking. However, his membership would be reviewed if he did not show the necessary improvement during that time.

* * * *

My international commitments were curtailed during 1978. My wife and I were expecting our first child, and I did not think it vital to travel to Jonquiere in Canada where the 1979 World Championships were to be held. The river race paddlers needed to go and learn their course at Desbiens (which was on a different river), but the slalom course was being remodelled at the end of 1978 with significant changes planned for the river bed. In addition, many of the European countries would be sending reduced teams because of the distance to Canada. Issues of 'jet lag', because of the time distance, and general disruption to training had to be considered as well. By 1979, there would be a 'new' river bed, and gate positions were not even on the agenda. It was more important for team management to go, and Albert Woods would be there to sort out any problems and pave the way for 1979. More importantly, I had to respect the goodwill shown by the College, and asked for leave of absence only when it was necessary. This was not one of my priority competitions.

1978 was a time of intense training within the Centre. Richard Fox travelled to Stone regularly, and stayed with Bill Berrisford's family. Liz Sharman drove from Bury St Edmunds for each training weekend, and usually stayed with the Baillie's in Eccleshall. (Alistair Baillie was a Centre member). The other members were able to travel daily. At one of the training weekends in Stone, Liz learnt the importance of concentration. The first session of the weekend was a straightforward run down a twenty gate course. However, I had said clearly, and emphasised the point, that anyone who hit a gate in this first run would not be able to continue with the rest of the training weekend. She hit the first gate! On her one hundred and fifty mile drive home she had time to consider how 'unfair' I had been, and how it had cost her petrol money, and how she had wasted a whole weekend for one gate. When we next met, I was a little apprehensive. How would she react? To her credit, she just said that it was better to hit a straightforward gate at a training weekend rather than after two years' training for a world championships. Over the years, the issue was raised again as an important lesson learned! Liz told several people that she thought I could be a 'bit of a bully' at times but was happy that she always knew where she stood when working with me. I think that was a compliment – in a strange sort of way.

I had become really interested in the psychology of coaching while following my Masters Degree at Liverpool. The general approach of many paddlers when doing 'gate practice' was to repeat sequences several times in order to improve performance. Mastery of a sequence often depended on trial and error. However, slalom competition depends on a paddler's ability to select the best route and approach to the course **while looking from the bank**. This aspect was very much neglected by most paddlers, even at the highest level, because it meant continually getting in and out of the boat. The **aim** of each session had to be decided in advance, because fitness, endurance and speed sessions sometimes conflicted with effective competition strategies. Liz had been found wanting on one occasion. It did not happen again. My insistence that paddlers, who hit a gate on a timed sequence, had to get out of the boat and look at the course from the bank may have been irksome at times, but this was what slalom involved!

* * * *

Richard Fox did not make the team for 1978. He may have been giving the necessary attention to studies he had neglected while competing and preparing for Spittal the previous year. For whatever reason, his performances did not reach the levels of 1977. The offer to move to Stone was still available, and, after complet-

119

ing his GCE 'A' levels, he asked if I would speak to his parents who needed assurance that a move north would be to his benefit. I was able to give them that assurance. The Berrisfords would provide accommodation. *I* could coach him **each** day – sometimes more if necessary. The Centre of Excellence was properly funded, **and** we could find employment if necessary. Furthermore, John MacLeod had made me aware of some discipline 'problems' that had occurred on the Youth Team Trip to Austria in the summer. I was working with students of sixteen to nineteen years of age at College, and envisaged no problems in that area.

Richard moved to Stone in September of 1978, and John Court arranged temporary employment for him – as a labourer, straightening scaffolding poles. After a couple of months of negotiations, John was able to obtain a grant that required Richard to undertake a study on the 'perceived needs, and provision for canoeing in Staffordshire'. I have no idea how he acquired the grant – but that was his strength! By the end of the year, Richard was a full time canoeist – and being paid.

* * * *

John Court, in his negotiations with Welsh Water, got permission for us to train on the River Clywedog, near Llanidloes. It meant arranging water releases, which he also managed to obtain without charge. This was one of our best sites – a narrow, fast flowing river on which gates could be easily erected and where we could train on technically demanding courses. Typical sessions would involve paddlers **self timing** their runs. Large kitchen clocks, with 'sweep' seconds hand, were sited at the top and bottom of the course. Paddlers started at minute intervals and were able to compare times with their **own** previous performances. It was not necessary to know anyone else's time because there was no knowledge of mistakes that another paddler had made, or how hard that paddler was trying. I was able to convince paddlers to learn the specific time differences in their individual alternative approaches to a specific sequence. The next stage was to get them to use their own stop watches to record their times, but to estimate their time **before looking at their watch**. The whole focus was to show each paddler how to evaluate his or her performance. In short, the aim was to teach paddlers to think.

The drive and determination of the squad at that time is best shown by the attitude to training weekends in bad weather. We had a weekend arranged at the Clywedog very early in the year when we managed to drive to Llanidloes but could not reach the training site because of snow on the road. A phone call to the Water Authority resulted in them sending one of their landrovers to guide us through a local caravan site and up to our training site. The weekend went as planned in sub-zero temperatures with thirty centimetres of snow on the ground. Video analysis produced scenes that would have been more appropriate on a Christmas card or in Arctic training with the armed forces!

* * * *

Back at Stone, I was able to coach Richard Fox several times each week. His organisation, record keeping and training diary were fundamental to his success. Often it would be his request for specific sessions that determined the programme. Sometimes, a pyramid session around a thirty second course of six gates would be physically demanding as one, two, four, and then eight laps of the course were followed by the four, two and then one lap. Controlled rest periods, pulse counting and consistency in the number of strokes were all monitored on different occasions. Then there were the technique sessions where a full one hour session could be spent discussing the best angle of the paddle blade and optimum distance from the boat to achieve maximum effect. Again, it was not myself telling Richard **how** to do something. It was more of a discussion where we were able to analyse and evaluate the effectiveness of different approaches. The aim of coaching is to encourage the paddler to think for themselves.

In some sports, this may not be necessary. The more formal and structured the techniques are in a sport, the more prescriptive the coach can be. In trampolining, archery or similar sports, the coach can be more dictatorial. However, as a former national judo coach expressed so clearly,- "If you see a move, you've missed it!" What he was saying is that, in his sport, speed of response is so fast that it is very much sub-conscious. Canoe slalom is like this. All a coach can do is teach the paddler to read the situation correctly, select the correct course of action and perform it efficiently in response to the demands of that situation. It sounds quite simple but there is a bit more to consider than this. If paddlers are to learn how to read situations correctly, the coach must create situations that are both relevant and appropriate. The sequences must be **realistic** and comparable to those that paddlers would face in international competition. The slalom course must be at the centre of training. It has to be adjusted properly, with poles at the correct heights. Even now, twenty-five years later, I am amazed by the number of paddlers who train without first adjusting poles to the same height they expect to face in competition.

After the performance, the paddler needs to be able to analyse it – by making use of all the additional feedback available from split times, video and his own mental recall. At the highest level, the coach keeps a very low profile in the competitive situation – restricting himself to maintaining a supportive and positive environment. He remains very much in the background, taking notes of how his paddlers performed and identifying issues that can be addressed back in the training environment. The coach can learn as much about a paddler's level of confidence by what he does **not** say and, also, by the questions he does **not** ask. There are times when a paddler asks for advice just to take the pressure off themselves. It means someone else can be blamed if a strategy does not work! This is frequently an undervalued role of the coach.

* * * *

Throughout the first winter that Richard lived in Stone, there was ample opportunity to work closely with him. Routine and **regular** 'periodic' training was important. It had always been important to cover the miles on the canal that would provide basic endurance, and then increase the amount of speed training as the competitive season approached. Weight training, gymnasium work and a variety of other forms of physical activity supported work done in the boat. However, my philosophy was that **"all slalom training is remedial"**. This means the paddler concentrates on correcting faults that have been identified in competition. The bigger faults demand the greater priority in training.

Richard did not lack speed down the course. We knew this from his performance in the Grandtully slalom where he had been 'noticed' for the first time, and on subsequent occasions since then. His failure to be selected for the team in 1978 was solely because he incurred too many penalties. This had to be the focus of attention.

I had also recognised the obvious. **"A coach cannot watch a paddler thinking".** Any improvement in concentration depended on discussions between us. Different strategies had to be tried, discussed and evaluated.

Starting with basic sequences, much work was done on comparing different ways of paddling the same sequence of three or four gates. Comparing the time difference between a 'tight' approach to an upstream gate (where the boat covered a shorter distance but lost all speed on the gate line), and a 'wide approach where speed was maintained but the boat travelled a greater distance, gave a greater understanding of where time could be saved or lost. I even used a stop watch to **quantify** the difference between approaches. Once all possible options had been tried – even those that would normally be dismissed without a second thought, we moved down to the next sequence. Eventually, we had an optimum time for each sequence which, when added together, gave a target time for the full course. Richard now had to get as close to the optimum time for each sequence when paddled as a full run.

After such sessions, the different approaches would be rated as 'safe' or 'risky'. Sometimes, the fastest option would be discarded because it was not safe enough to use in competition. Gradually, though, practice using this principle changed 'risky' approaches into 'safe' ones. More importantly, Richard was able to assess how much time would be lost by 'playing it safe'.

There were other sessions where he would inspect a prepared course before getting on the water, complete his warm-up above the start, and do two or three runs at competition speed – equating to the practice run and the two competition runs at a major event. The rest of the session would be spent breaking the course into sequences that were then practised individually to see where improvements could have been made. Finally, another full run would show the effectiveness of his original strategy for tackling the course. If he improved, his initial tactics were not good enough. If he didn't improve he was not fit enough. I always won!

Over a six month period, courses increased from thirty to fifty or sixty gates. Thirty gates were marked with poles, the other thirty were positions where he needed to put the boat to be 'safe' – safe enough to guarantee a clear run. His motto –'fast and clean' – soon became his trade mark.

At training events away from Stone, and at national team weekends, Richard's ability to 'read' the course carried on improving. I needed to say absolutely nothing to him. My role was to design courses that required paddlers to make decisions. The more options that I could build into a course, the more likely it was that paddlers would get into the 'mind set' of the course designer. It was possible, and quite common, to position a gate in such a way that a paddler would be penalised, not on that gate but two or three gates later – because he or she ran out of space. Such a principle is well known in ski slalom course design.

In ski slalom, despite its strenuous nature, speed down the course is provided by gravity and determined by the quality of the wax used on the skis. In slalom canoeing, greater physical effort is required by the paddler. It is not possible to put in maximum effort throughout the length of the course, and he must decide where that effort is best directed.

Maximum effort, by its definition, means that a paddler cannot accelerate to change direction and get out of trouble. He can only brake, which loses time. Working at sub- maximal level gives a greater degree of control, which is obviously more important when **approaching** a gate, because being out of position will incur gate penalties as well as loss of time. My approach focused on the optimum **exit** from the gate. Three factors were important; speed across the gate line, angle of the boat in the gate and the amount of rotation on the gate line. It all depended on the position of the next two or three gates on the course. Allowing the boat to slow down on the approach to the gate made it easier to position it for the best exit, and, as a paddler needed to pace himself throughout the length of the course, this was the best place to 'ease off'.

Eventually, it was a straightforward task to ignore the boat and the paddler and watch the paddler's crash helmet instead. Slowing down approaching the gate was usually correct. Accelerating away from the gate was essential.

There were many more 'principles' that were applied. All focused on reducing the likelihood of penalties. Underpinning everything was discussion and evaluation of lessons learnt. This was very much a two way process, and an intensive six months where I learnt as much as he did.

* * * *

It might seem that Richard had more time allocated to him than to other Centre paddlers – to their detriment. In fact a situation had arisen at training weekends where I often used him to demonstrate a point that I needed to make. Unfortunately, I had overlooked **his** needs and was in danger of passing all **his** understanding and knowledge to those competing against him! He told me that he was not happy, and that it was a bit unfair.

I had to agree. It was just my insensitive side coming out again! The outcome was that I spent more time with Richard **away** from training weekends, and left him alone at training weekends while I worked with the rest of the Centre members.

As he became more aware of his own needs, Richard had a much greater input to the weekend programmes. He **knew** what he needed – much more than most other paddlers – and was sufficiently articulate and organised to ask well in advance of each weekend.

* * * *

Selection for the Jonquiere World Championships soon came around in 1979. Bill Berrisford had made massive strides in C1 during the winter. The absence of competitions in the second half of 1978 had prevented him from being promoted above Division Three, but I was convinced he was in the top three paddlers in the country on ability. I submitted an application on his behalf that he should be allowed to enter the selection events that were held in conjunction with Premier Division slaloms at the beginning of 1979. I made the point that we needed to send the best team, and that nobody should be denied the opportunity to represent their country because they had improved at a faster rate than the Divisional System could accommodate. Questions were asked. Was he being able to take part just because he was a member of the West Midlands Centre of Excellence? It was finally accepted that anyone who was of the appropriate standard should be allowed to represent the country. Selection was not being made on Premier Division rankings but on the performance in a specific event. If he was not good enough, this would be obvious in that event. Bill was allowed to take part in Selection events as a Division Three paddler, and qualified on paddling merit. He was selected.

* * * *

It was a real surprise to many people that Bill Berrisford had been able to develop as a C1 so quickly, and this possibly needs an explanation.

Canadian paddlers used one blade and had an individual preference as either a 'lefty' or a 'righty'. I had always needed to address this issue when designing courses. 'Lefties' were considered to have the advantage on left handed breakouts, because they could 'pull' the boat into the eddy and support it on the downstream side as they crossed the eddy line into the main current after negotiating an upstream gate. 'Righties' had a similar 'advantage' on right hand break outs. The belief was that, if a course was to be fair to both lefties and 'righties', it would have an equal number of lefty and righty moves. I had first experienced this situation in 1969 when competing at Augsburg – prior to the Bourg St. Maurice World Championships. The **eiskanal** was about ten metres wide and a metre deep with a flat concrete bed. Two telegraph poles, fixed across the bed of this channel, formed a 'stopper' wave that extended three quarters of its width. A gate had been positioned on the right, two metres above the stopper. The next gate was two metres below the stopper, on the left. This resulted in a 'righty' move – because the right handed paddler could support his boat with the blade on his downstream side as he traversed the stopper from right to left. I had a discussion with Mike Hillyard, one of the British 'lefty' paddlers, who complained that the course was unfair because they were losing between five and ten seconds on this single sequence. He could not agree with my assertion that paddlers should change sides for this move, and defended his position that paddlers are either lefties or righties. I failed to understand his contention that, if courses were 'balanced', it would even itself out. Nowhere in the rules were canadian paddlers 'forced' to paddle on one side only – but most of them did!

In the Centre, twenty years later, we were working with Bill Berrisford on his technique. In training, he would paddle sequences as a 'lefty' **and** as a 'righty'. We could then quantify the time he could save by 'switching' his blade at specific points down a course. Bill, and Pete Bell, became recognised 'switchers' and became established international paddlers because of it.

There is a **much** stronger case to be made for the canadian doubles having 'balanced' courses. In the traditional C2, the **highest** parts of the boat had to be within thirty centimetres of each end. There was no realistic possibility of the boat passing under a slalom pole, and paddlers sat towards the ends to give greater leverage when changing direction. In the early seventies, the relaxation of the 'ends rule', as it was called, led to new designs where paddlers sat close to the centre of the boat and could pass broadside through a gate as the lowered ends slipped under the poles. Because they were now positioned at the widest part of the boat, cockpits needed to be 'offset' to enable paddlers to execute the full range of strokes. Consequently, although C1's could become switchers, it was more difficult for the C2's.

* * * *

Although Richard Fox did not make the senior team for 1978, the time spent training at Stone had been very productive. He qualified easily for the 1979 World championships and joined Nicky Wain, Alan Edge and Albert Kerr at Merano as part of the 'warm up' programme prior to our departure to Canada.

Merano sits on the River Passer which flows through the centre of the town. Four metre high walls, fifty metres apart, contain the river early in the year and prevent Spring floods surging through the town. By the middle of June, water levels have usually subsided, and new rapids are formed as the river flows over constantly shifting shingle banks that change each year. The river, upstream of the first road bridge, the Postbrücke, had slow moving flat water either side of a series of standing waves. There was no specific eddy for upstream gate 14, and the water flowed slowly **downstream** through it. Albert Kerr was powerful enough to pull his boat in behind the gate and paddle through it in three strokes. Everyone else was taking four, five or six strokes and losing seconds. There was a gap of a metre between the gate and the bank, and I suggested that paddlers ought to try driving towards the bank **above** the gate, crossing the gate line with the boat parallel to the bearer wire and **pushing** the stern of the boat under the bank side pole while the paddler leant backwards and passed between gate and bank.. The paddler would then finish much higher behind the gate and at the correct angle to drive across the gate line into the main current. We tried the manoeuvre and found it to be about three seconds quicker. After the session, we tried not to practise the move too often, in case other nations saw us. In the actual event, few people tried it, but the British paddlers were three seconds quicker on this move – a fact noted by other teams, who used it on their second runs. In subsequent training weekends and in competition, the 'Merano' became the term used for this move.

* * * *

The team for Jonquiere also included Graham Helsby, who had a brilliant run in selection to put out more fancied paddlers. However, there were no complaints. The selection had been open and fair and a strong team of four mens K1, three C1's and three ladies K1 was selected. Jim Sibley went as C1 coach. Ray Calverley and myself were the kayak coaches and Albert Woods was again the Team Manager. Graham Mackereth arranged for the team boats to be shipped over to Canada in a thirty foot container which remained on site for the duration of the event, and which was regarded by other teams as the British boat store. In fact, Pyranha supplied boats for several teams and almost a third of the men's kayaks used them. Albert Woods had also organised a thirty five foot caravan to be delivered to the site for us to use as a base (because the nearest town was several miles away).This caused considerable discomfort to other teams whose paddlers questioned their 'team management' into why the British Team seemed to be far better serviced than they were.

129

The level of confidence in the team was extremely high. Albert Kerr was World Champion, but we now had three paddlers who, on their day, were as good as him. In the ladies event, Liz Sharman was British Champion and producing really good international results. Peter Keane and Martyn Hedges had both won international competitions in 1977 and were serious medal contenders here too.

* * * *

The Jonquiere World Championships were a significant point in the development of slalom because, for the first time, the event was taking place **outside** Europe. German, French and Italian had been the dominant languages of the host nations in previous championships. Now, the language used would be English. The 'official' team leaders' meetings were in English, French and German, but obtaining extra resources, such as our caravan (which was more like a mobile home), the hire of vehicles, and day to day organisation of accommodation and meals, was now easier for us. It was the European countries who were now at a disadvantage – even if it was a minor one, remembering that Canadians speak French and English in this part of Quebec, and most are bi-lingual.

The West Midlands Centre of Excellence was represented by Liz Sharman, Bill Berrisford, Jane Roderick and Richard Fox – four of the ten competitors. Each had developed significantly in the two years that the centre had existed. It was not necessary to establish working relationships – as had always been necessary at previous events. I was working regularly with these paddlers. I had worked regularly with Nicky Wain and Alan Edge as team members since before Skopje, four years earlier.The relationships already existed and just needed to be maintained. Consequently, the atmosphere was relaxed and positive. Richard Fox had reached the stage where he certainly did not need to speak to me for advice. He was fully able to evaluate his own needs. My involvement with the three team event paddlers was more on the aspects of 'team work' in the team event – checking that each person knew their role, the spacing between each paddler, and giving information on how their performance looked from the bank. With Graham Helsby it was different. He had been selected on an outstanding performance at one event and needed the confidence to demonstrate that this was a standard he could produce again. In short, his mental state was more 'fragile' because he did not have the **habit** of successful international performance. My focus in the individual events was more to support him. The other men's kayaks could look after themselves, and would come to me only if they identified an issue that needed to be addressed. I did not think this situation would arise.

In the individual events for men's kayak, Albert Kerr was given a debateable penalty on his first run which deprived him of a silver medal. Our team video showed the judge had made a mistake, but video was not admissible evidence and our official protest was rejected, which left him in ninth place. Richard Fox finished third, but his bronze medal was accompanied by disappointment because he knew he could have done even better. Alan Edge's fifteenth place suggested that a medal was certainly possible in the team event, athough individual results of first, second and fourth made the Austrians favourite for the gold.

On the second day, it was the turn of the ladies and canadian singles. Liz Sharman took the Silver Medal in the ladies, and Peter Keane in seventh place was the best result by any British C1 at a world championships. Furthermore, we had for the first time taken two medals at a World Championships. I reminded Liz of the time I had sent her home from that training weekend in Stone. She just smiled.

The third day was reserved for team events. Bill Berrisford really justified his selection as the C1's finished just outside the medals in fourth place. The ladies, too, just missed out and also took the unenviable fourth place in their class.

The men's kayak team event was the last event where we could take a medal. I had always felt that team event paddling was much more than three individual performances – which was why I believed that more team event medals would have been won if the Manchester A Team had been able to contest the world championships with Dave Mitchell competing as fourth man, even though he was undoubtedly the best *individual* paddler. Juergen Bremer had won *his* first world championship in 1963 while paddling as fourth man! We had spent a great deal of time with Albert Kerr, Alan Edge and Richard Fox trying to add 'team work' into the individual skills they obviously had. All had been top ten paddlers in world championships.

Alan Edge was undoubtedly the slowest of the three paddlers, and years later he reminded me of what I had said prior to the team runs. In effect, I said that because he *was* the slowest, he should have priority over the other two. They would keep out of his way. They could work round him. All he needed to do was produce a solid clean run ignoring them completely! He interpreted this to mean that it all depended on him as the weakest link!! No pressure at all!

The British Team was last down the course on their second run, and tried to avoid everyone as they waited. It was important that they did not know how other teams had done because this would increase pressure, and because it was irrelevant. They were in control of their own performance and were competing against the course, not against anybody else. I just waited at the start while they completed their warm up well above the course, as I usually did in case a paddle broke or running repairs were needed. My only signal was a thumbs up sign to ask if everything was all right. Alan returned the sign. No words were spoken.

Alan handled the pressure. The team were brilliant and took the gold medal. The Austrians who had been favourites, and who were obviously disappointed, were first to offer congratulations.

Britain had taken three medals. Albert Kerr had taken his second gold medal. Richard Fox took two medals at the same championships. Liz Sharman took our first medal in Ladies K1. A team of ten paddlers was returning with five medals. The slalom world championships had expanded outside its European boundaries.

* * * *

At the end of 1979, with the next world championships allocated to Bala, North Wales, I stepped down from coaching the national team after fifteen years working at this level. In 1963, the East Germans (DDR) had asked for an extra minute in the start intervals because they were following the British! In the fifteen years that followed, we had raised the standard of our performance to among the best in the world. We had finally laid to rest the notion of 'gallant losers'.

Every nation that staged a world championships needed to provide someone for the Course Design Commission that would design, maintain and oversee the course for the duration of the event. I was the **only** member of the Team Management Group who was coaching at international level and who was also an ICF qualified judge. In addition, my involvement and interest in course design for more than fifteen years made me an obvious choice for the Commission. In fact, there was no choice!

John MacLeod took over the task of working with the kayaks, and the BCU National Coaching and Development Committee, in conjunction with the Slalom Committee, appointed Hugh Mantle as National Slalom Coach to develop a 'structured system of club and squad coaches' to assist slalomists.

Hugh brought a new dimension to coaching. Although not a slalomist, his expertise in sports psychology would sit well alongside the technical aspects of slalom paddling that John MacLeod could contribute.

* * * *

1980 was a strange year for me. Many things had changed. I was still attending team training weekends, especially when they were held at Bala. It was important that all possible sequences of gates had been tried and tested. The World Championships were eighteen months away and I felt it necessary to keep my distance from the National Slalom Squad to ensure impartiality. When we had competed at Lipno in 1967, there had been mutterings that the Czech & DDR teams seemed to have been practising sequences in the preceding months that were very close to the actual course used for the world championships. Nothing could be proved and no action was taken, but suspicions remained. The difficulty in obtaining visas to enter Czechoslovakia and train on the course prior to those championships, and the continued non-availability of water releases from the dam, did little to allay those suspicions.

* * * *

Specifically, I would not be travelling to international competitions including the Europa Cup and the Pre-World Championships as team coach. Of course, I would be in Bala, but in an organisational capacity. Not travelling with the team was not a big issue. My coaching philosophy was to teach paddlers to think for themselves, make their *own* decisions, complete their own mental preparation and evaluate their own performances. I would produce courses that would make them think! There were enough other coaches available who would provide the necessary feedback from which each paddler could evaluate their performance.

* * * *

At the National Canoe Exhibition, held in February at Crystal Palace, I was presented with the British Canoe Union Award of Merit for services to canoeing over the previous fifteen years. Although much appreciated, it did seem like the kind of award given to people when they retired. I was certainly not retiring!

* * * *

The plan for 1980 included competition at Zwickau, East Germany. However, teams could only compete if they were formally 'invited' into the country – which meant they could get the necessary visas. We were aware of the gradual withdrawal of funding from non-Olympic sports in the DDR, and canoe slalom had slipped into that category. Perhaps our success in Jonquiere was seen as a threat to their chances of success at this event. Perhaps it was an administrative oversight. Whatever the reason, we were not invited, and competed at Monschau, West Germany, instead.

It was probably a good decision, because the men's K1 paddlers took 2nd, 4th, 5th and 6th, the ladies 1st and 4th; the C1's 1st, 2nd and 3rd, and C2's 4th, 5th and 6th places. As a confidence booster, it was excellent. The only danger now was complacency. Since I did not travel, it was pleasing to see Pete Bell, who had developed as a Centre member, get a silver medal. Liz was **expected** to medal because she had become a hardened competitor and was able to focus well on the event, but Jane Roderick had also continued her progress from Jonquiere. Her fourth place was less important than the fact that she was now 'on the pace'.

The three Europa Cup events were Merano in Italy, Beuil-Sur-Roya in southern France and Seu d'Urgell in the Spanish Pyrenees. Richard Fox finished 11th, 1st and 7th. Liz Sharman had three second places, being beaten by Ulrike Deppe, of West Germany, on each occasion. The star performer was Martyn Hedges, who won all his three events – beating the seemingly invincible USA paddlers, who had been so dominant in Jonquiere. Even more significant was the success of the C2 team in the event at Beuil. Their gold medal was evidence of the progress they had made in the period they were denied access to World Championships. There would **definitely** be C2 representation in Bala.

The British Slalom Team had finished in second place, behind West Germany, in the Europa Cup. Four gold, six silver and five bronze medals showed the rest of the world that we were to be taken **very** seriously.

* * * *

In 1981, it was the Czech coach, Tibor Sykora, and Sue Chamberlain, from the USA, who would be working with me on the three man Course Design Commission. I had been designing courses in the UK for seventeen or eighteen years and selecting teams to compete at international and world championship events. For much of this time I was also a competitor and coach, and had worked hard to ensure that I was as impartial as possible, maintaining the confidentiality of committees on which I served. There was no chance that this situation would be compromised by accusations from visiting teams that I had been underhand or unfair. Instead, I spent many hours designing the greatest number of alternative sequences that could constitute a 'fair' course. I built up files of courses that were balanced with equal numbers of right and left hand moves so the canadian paddlers would not be able to say a course favoured left handers rather than right handers (or vice versa). My aim was to exhaust all possibilities before the World Championships and then be able to offer various balanced sequences, so that the other two members of the Commission would make the final decisions. The actual course would not matter to British paddlers because all possible sequences would have been tried and tested. Sequences where boat damage might occur were avoided. If not, they would have been eliminated at the team managers meeting that takes place after official practice runs and prior to the start of actual competition at any international event. Managers cannot ask for a change to a gate on the course because they do not like it! They have to give a reason – such as danger to paddler, unfair bias, boat damage, not wide enough for C2's, risk of catching blades on rocks, etc. The list is endless. However, no manager wants to change the course after practice – when his or her paddlers have successfully completed the sequence and taken the necessary video. It is only when 'problems' are identified, and **agreed** by a majority of team managers, that a decision is made to change the course. The credibility of a course designer depends to a large extent on its acceptance by competitors **without change**. Pride is at stake here!

Stafford and Stone Canoe Club were closely involved too. The slalom poles and gates were made by George Clough and a team of helpers from the club. The course erection and maintenance team were also from the club and over the year leading to the championships, the expertise in erecting, adjusting and maintaining courses became almost clinical in its efficiency.

* * * *

Mike Briggs from Chester, whose son Steve had been a top slalomist, took control of the slalom organisation, and put his own job on hold for the period leading up to the main event. The overall controller of operations was Stan Cooper who was allowed a period of sabbatical leave from the Army to concentrate full time on organising both slalom and white water racing events. I was still working full time at Stafford College and needed to re-schedule my activities!

I was approaching the end of my Masters Degree at Liverpool, which I had undertaken on a part time basis over the previous two years, and applied for leave of absence to do **another** masters degree. Keele University offered a degree in research methodology, and I was able to extend my studies in psychology by looking at issues related to motivation. I had been vaguely interested in finding out why many sports people, and many of those involved in outdoor activities, did not take part in 'competition'. I had attended a conference of the National Association of Outdoor Education some years earlier and was surprised by the number of people who thought competition put a block on their activities. Potholers, rock-climbers and mountaineers found enough challenge in mastering skills and dealing with 'real' challenges, and had no need of formal competition. I was also aware that many children are organised into competitive teams before acquiring the necessary skills to perform effectively.

I would be 'free' to schedule my studies around the demands of preparing for the Bala World Championships. Leave of absence was granted and I became a full time student again in July 1980! I submitted the title of my dissertation as "The place of Competitive Sport in Physical Education". Six or seven hours of formal lectures, split over two days each week, gave me the time to work on the dissertation and the flexibility to be at Bala and be involved in preparations.

A 'temporary' scaffolding bridge was built towards the end of the slalom course, but was made permanent by the weight of concrete bags used to secure the base! Moving rocks in the river bed and pruning trees to improve visability and facilitate course erection were among the many jobs that Mike and his team undertook – which made my job easier. I was able to spend complete days mapping the course and the trees, and planning even more gate sequences!

* * * *

Back in Stone, coaching within the Centre of Excellence was now much easier.

There were more additions to the group including Steve Parsonage, Mike Druce, Graham Gladwin and his brother, Andrew. Melvin Jones joined soon after. The majority were also members of the canoe club. Stafford and Stone Canoe Club had ten of the sixty Premier Division paddlers by the end of 1981. Liz Sharman, Sue Garriock and Jane Roderick also joined the club, as did Pete Bell and Dennis Hennesey. Andy Hawkesford and Phil Barber joined as C2 paddlers. It was a strong training group. One notable addition was Shane Kelly who came over from Ireland, and spent some time living in Stone and training with the squad. It caused something of a stir when he took first place at the Pre-World Championships at Bala in 1980, but it did suggest that we were doing most things right! He then returned to Dublin ready to come back in 1981.

John Court was still chasing funding because the group had expanded. Then, Tony Arrowsmith, from Warwickshire, applied to the West Midlands Sports Council for funding of a separate Centre of Excellence – on the basis that the Stone Centre of Excellence did not fully serve the needs of top paddlers **through-out** the West Midlands. Its location in the north of the region denied paddlers from Warwickshire and Worcester the opportunities available in North Staffordshire. In their perceived wisdom, the Sports Council divided the funding between the two disparate groups. John wrote to the West Midlands Sports Council explaining that we were meeting all the aims that Dennis Howell had sought when proposing the idea of Centres, stating that our success would be compromised by a drastic cut in funding. He reinforced the case by explaining that we were supplying a large proportion of the paddlers for national teams. In retrospect this was a mistake. The Sports Council said that if there were so many of our paddlers in the national teams, they should be funded from a national budget and not from a 'regional' grant. The success of the Centre was now seriously compromised and needed to continue solely on the funding that John could obtain through sponsorship. The momentum was maintained.

Coaching continued with all squad members, although Hugh Mantle was working much more closely with the men's kayaks – especially on their mental preparation. John MacLeod, Hugh Mantle and the other coaches continued to work with paddlers at team weekends. I was much more involved in providing the specific courses that the squad used.

* * * *

Time passed quickly, and soon it was July 1981. The world championships were here!

I am still convinced that, of all the people who worked to deliver a high quality world championship event, Mike Briggs received the least recognition for his contribution. He virtually lived on the site and was invaluable in getting the most important part of the competition ready – the course! I produced a detailed map of the river with rocks, eddies and the direction of flow marked. This was reduced to A4 size so that all teams could have several copies on which to mark gates and practice courses. When the other two members of the Course Commission arrived at the start of the championships, we spent several days watching paddlers as they tried different moves. Training gates were put up by Stafford and Stone Canoe Club and changed each day. Several nations had brought their own training gates and used them to supplement those we had provided. Every possible eddy was tried and tested and I was confident that nobody had come up with a feasible sequence that was not already in my file!

Then it was time to close the river to all competitors for the course to be designed. I walked the course with my two Commission members and discussions followed about possible sequences. I could intervene and say a specific move was not possible because the stern might be damaged or because there was insufficient depth for a C2 blade. Inevitably, a course was agreed. I had offered suggestions but avoided the final decisions for most of the time. There was **nothing** that was unexpected – at least to the British.

The course was published and each nation received several copies – on the same outline map that had been issued earlier in the week. There were no objections, and comments received were generally favourable. After demonstration runs and official practice, team managers met to approve the course. There were no changes! The competition could start. My job was done and I was now a spectator – unless the course fell down!

* * * *

The men's kayaks began proceedings on the Wednesday. At the end of first runs Richard Fox was fastest by almost three seconds – which was no real surprise to me – but he picked up sixty penalties, leaving him in 39th place. Lubos Hilgert had the fastest clean run and was in the lead. Albert Kerr was only one second slower but had fifteen penalties, and an eskimo roll, leaving him in eighth place. Nicky Wain and Jim Dolan also picked up penalties, but Nicky was still in the top ten.

John MacLeod took Richard away prior to second runs so that nobody could find him. This was the tactic the team had used in Jonquiere. The performance of other paddlers did not matter at all. It was Richard against the course. Well meaning supporters are always willing to give information about the performance of the opposition, in the mistaken belief that it will provide some kind of encouragement. The reality is different. John would protect him from absolutely everybody. Richard would relax and then refocus. It was well into the second runs before he paddled down towards the start. The crowd were surprisingly quiet, as if they knew the importance of the next three and a half minutes. Once he left the start, everything changed as a crowd of a hundred or so supporters increased to two hundred and made the noise of five hundred. I could see small mistakes where he needed to make minor adjustments, but there was no real time loss until he approached the last gate and had to make a massive correction stroke in order to avoid a penalty. Usually, a paddler of his stature knew when he had completed a really good run, but Richard was very quiet as he pulled into the bank. Even after the last competitor had completed the course, it took a few minutes before the result was announced. No time was given and no name mentioned when the announcer started speaking. It might as well have been a public service announcement – "Ladies and Gentleman ....the Champion of the World is Richard Fox". The time and penalties were lost in the eruption of sound across the site.

I was totally emotional. Albert Kerr's gold medal four year's earlier had been completely unexpected. There was no tension and no suspense. It just happened and turned quickly into celebration. This was different. Richard was the favourite and it was **his** gold medal to lose. The years of analysing technique and stroke efficiency had paid off. He had now moved on and would seldom need to return to me again for advice.

Nicky Wain was eighth and Jim Dolan tenth. We had three paddlers in the top ten.

Next came the canadian doubles. Britain entered three crews who finished sixth, twelfth and eighteenth – a big improvement on the performance of eight years earlier when C2's had taken three of the last four places. Major strides had been made and these paddlers were here on merit and not just to make up the numbers.

On the Thursday it was the turn of the ladies. Ulrike Deppe, from West Germany, took gold. Liz Sharman was fast enough to win, but penalties on each run left her in fifteenth place – disappointing after her silver medal in Jonquiere. The best performance in the ladies was Jane Roderick, who finished tenth and who was a fully fledged member of the Centre of Excellence in Stone.

In the C1 event, in Jonquiere, the USA paddlers had been totally dominant and continued that trend by taking four of the top six places in Bala. Fourth place by Martyn Hedges and seventh for Peter Keane were brilliant performances in this company. The results of each of the top ten paddlers in this class were good enough to have put any one of them on the rostrum in the ladies event.

Friday was team event day. The men's kayaks took the gold again, which meant Nicky Wain, who narrowly missed out in selection for the 1979 championships, had his gold medal. Albert Kerr had now won gold at three consecutive world championships. His achievement had been phenomenal, but Richard Fox had 'done the double' of individual and team, which was immediately recognised by the spectators. It overshadowed Albert's performance – and continued to do so in the days and weeks of media coverage that followed. Albert never received appropriate recognition for his achievements.

The ladies took the silver medal in their team event, which was some consolation to Liz Sharman. Sue Small and Jane Roderick completed the team.

In the canadian doubles team event, Britain was just out of the medal positions at the end of first runs by less than a fifth of a second. On their second run, they posted the fastest time of the day with just thirty five seconds of penalties to take a totally unexpected gold medal. Maybe my objections after the performances in 1973, when I had advocated not sending any C2's to world championships until the standard improved, had been vindicated. Maybe the class could have been re-introduced earlier. We will never know. However, in the intervening years, the standard **had** risen to world level.

In the C1's, the team of Keane, Hedges and Berrisford missed out again, taking fourth place as they had done two years earlier.

The medal haul had exceeded that of 1979.

* * * *

My year's sabbatical was now over and I needed to complete my dissertation and return to College lecturing to catch up on developments, and apply the fruits of my studies. Somehow, I was now out of the coaching equation – at least as far as the national team was concerned. Hugh Mantle was even more involved with coaching the men's kayaks at team weekends. I returned to coaching members of the Centre of Excellence, and focused on the new courses that I was now teaching. The college was receiving requests for 'team building courses' and the academic side had new developments in Recreation and Leisure. I was busier than I had ever been, and canoeing had to take second place – probably for the first time in several years!

By July of 1982, I had a first degree, two Masters' degrees and a Teacher's Certificate. I really needed to do more with them! I now had a daughter who was three months old and a son who, at the age of four, deserved much more of my time.

* * * *

In Stone, an atmosphere of confidence permeated the club. I had stepped back from 'front line' coaching. Centre paddlers became club paddlers. Ten of the top men's kayaks in the country now trained at Stone. Melvyn Jones, who had been promoted to Premier Division at the end of 1981, joined them. Three of the top four ladies, and three C1,s from the top division completed the group.

The absence of funding for the Centre of Excellence reduced the number of organised activities, but this did not matter now. When a group of paddlers have this amount of momentum, it is often better to step back and let things happen. The competitive atmosphere blended in well with a spirit of co-operation. Paul McConkey was determined to beat Richard's time for the run to the Trent Road bridge and back down the A34 to the training site. Other paddlers had their own rivalries. I started distance running, a phase that was to last about four years, competing in London, New York, the Lake District and Snowdonia marathons – several with Jon Goodwin. There were longer races of fifty miles and more in the Peak District. For me, it was a chance to do something different for a while. I even had a couple of seasons playing third and fourth team rugby for Stoke on Trent RUFC.

Throughout this time, I continued my involvement in course design. In fact, I probably became more active in this area. I still coached but not as much as before.

* * * *

In 1983, World Championships came around again, and were held in Merano. I had been to the ten previous championships – either as paddler or coach. These were the first I had missed since 1963. However, I knew paddlers from the club were as well prepared as possible. They were independent and experienced. Besides, I had just purchased a plot of land and was busy building my own house!

Liz Sharman took gold, which gave me great pleasure, and the satisfaction of a third world champion who had come through the Centre and with whom I had been closely involved as coach. John MacLeod phoned me with the results and I admit to being completely speechless – which anyone who knew me would have found hard to believe! Richard Fox took the individual gold – again. He, with fellow club member Paul McConkey and Jim Dolan from Manchester, took gold in the team event. Liz Sharman, Jane Roderick and Sue Garriock, all from the club, took team silver.

The icing on the cake was that, by 1983, Stafford and Stone Canoe Club members had taken more medals in world championship events than the rest of the Great Britain team, put together, since the first championships were held in 1949.

* * * *

The Committee running the canoe club was under the dynamic chairmanship of Phil Baskerville. In addition to playing a major role in the organisation of club events, he and his committee had been negotiating for the erection of a clubhouse on the site at Stone. The possibility of building *our own* clubhouse was rejected by the members in favour of an attractive offer from Stafford Borough Council, who agreed to provide a building that we could lease. The project was completed by 1981, and we made the first payment in January 1984. The club now had boat and equipment storage, a club room, changing rooms and all the necessary facilities for running slaloms.

The bandwagon continued to roll and, by 1984, Stafford and Stone Canoe Club could rightly claim to be 'undisputed' best slalom club in Great Britain – ever! If there *had* been claims from any other club, the evidence was overwhelming in our favour. Six of the top twelve top men's kayak paddlers came from the club – most of it 'home grown' talent that had risen through the Centre of Excellence. The top three ladies in Britain all paddled for the club. In C1, Pete Bell was ranked second and there were two other canadians in the top division. Richard Fox had started a new magazine, which he edited from his flat on the Lichfield Road in Stone. *"Feedback"* was the first magazine specifically aimed at slalomists and their training.

In October, at the end of that year, Stafford and Stone Canoe Club ran the British Open event at Llangollen again, and played a major role in course erection and maintenance at the international on the following weekend – for which I, once again, designed the courses. Sponsorship of the event by Foster's Lager gave an added opportunity to celebrate the club's achievements – and its place at the pinnacle of the sport.

* * * *

In 1985, the club was, once again, well represented at international level. The Centre of Excellence had declined in importance and become virtually obsolete. Training centred on the new clubhouse, where Paul McConkey and Andrew (Wilbur) Willett had supervised the erection of floodlights on a hundred metre stretch of the slalom course. The attraction of the club increased with its improved training facilities.

In the World Championships, at Augsburg, Liz Sharman added a team bronze to her tally of medals, Richard Fox won his third individual gold medal, making him the most successful men's kayak paddler in the history of the sport. Once again, I did not attend.

At home, Jim Croft organised the first National Inter-clubs slalom competition on the artificial course at Cardington, Bedford. The format required each club to enter paddlers from all divisions – Novice to Premier, as well as representatives from ladies, C1 and C2. In short, it was a competition designed to measure strength in depth among all British clubs. Stafford and Stone Canoe Club won this inaugural event. Paul McConkey and Bill Berrisford paddled together in C2!

* * * *

At Nottingham, construction of an artificial slalom course on the Trent at Holme Pierrepont was nearing completion. The concept had been inspired by the course used at Augsburg for the 1972 Olympics. Continued pressure from many quarters, including Frank Goodman, of Valley Canoe Products, and George Parr, a hydrologist at Nottingham University, had turned a fourteen year dream into reality. Because of my interest in course design, I had been involved in the early committee stages when the project was known as A.S.C.O.T. (or Artificial Slalom Course on Trent). More recently, John MacLeod had been engaged in designing the gate erection and adjustment system that most paddlers still believe to be among the best in the world for its reliability and ease of operation.

When the course was officially opened by the Princess Royal, in the Summer of 1986, the face of British slalom canoeing changed forever. The implications for Stafford and Stone Canoe Club were equally profound – although it took time to take effect, and for members of the club to recognise it. At best, the focus of British slalom canoeing would move to this new facility in Nottingham. At worse, it would signal the end of Stafford and Stone as a major force in the slalom world.

I was concerned and, although I had stepped back from any organisational role in the club, I started to 'interfere'. The success of Richard Fox was a double edged sword. On the positive side, it 'opened doors' by raising the status of the club within the community. Richard was invited to officially open the new sports centre at Westbridge Park, close to the canoe club. The club was more likely to be consulted when any significant change was planned in the local area, which might impinge on club activities. On the negative side, some members still believed the club was unstoppable and would continue its progress unchecked. However, I had experienced, at first hand, the case of Manchester Canoe Club which tried, unsuccessfully, in the seventies to live on its reputation from the sixties. I was also aware of the decline in fortunes of Chalfont Park Canoe Club which had been the most successful club in the fifties. We **needed** to change to survive.

All paddlers who had aspirations for international representation moved to Nottingham if they could. Nottingham and Nottingham Trent Universities became desirable places to study. Paddlers set up home or shared flats and bed-sits in Great Bridgeford, and a whole new canoeing community spawned into existence.

I was probably more concerned than I needed to be. We still had the best midweek training gates because, unlike Nottingham, we had floodlights, and paddlers could train throughout the winter. Unlike Nottingham, we had a clubhouse **and** a club atmosphere. I had been too involved at international level to recognise the simple enjoyment that many club paddlers get from just being on the water.

One such club paddler was Donald Bean, who I first met when he joined the 'Men's Keep Fit' evening class, that I ran at the College, in Stafford, for almost twenty years. Donald entered competitions, but was totally non-competitive. He was a bachelor who worked in the County Treasurer's Department. As an insomniac, who seldom slept more than three or four hours each night, he was an active yoga participant, and kept two allotments. He grew fruit and made jam which he sold – and then gave the proceeds of his sales to boost club funds. He had been a recreational canoeist since the late 1930's and still helped local scout troops with their canoeing. He even did their financial accounts at the end of each year – free of charge.

Donald entered slaloms and got a great deal of satisfaction when he beat someone – anyone! Yet such people are the lifeblood of a club, and, with his generosity in providing canoes for the club on a regular basis, the club would continue – and prosper. All he asked for in return was the friendship of those in the club, **and** that all the boats he provided should be yellow with the initials 'DB1' on the bow. Soon there were a lot of yellow boats in the club!

* * * *

At the start of 1986 Pat Thorn decided he no longer had the time to work as a national team coach with the C2's at international level. Alan Edge asked me if I would be willing to take on the task. I needed to give this some serious thought. I had been **very** vociferous in my opposition to the selection of C2's for world championships in the seventies, which I still felt was the correct decision. I had also stated that I felt many canadian paddlers had taken up the discipline because they could not make the national team in kayaks. Although this had changed, and Peter Keane, Martin Hedges, and the C2 paddlers in the World Championships at Bala and Merano had sh.wn that British canadian paddlers could hold their own against any international competition, there was still a worry, on my part, that I would not be welcome.

I accepted the task and travelled to Bourg St. Maurice for the 1986 Pre-World Championships as C2 team coach. I need not have been concerned about relationships with the paddlers, who were glad to have a coach working specifically with them. My approach was no different than it had been when working with kayaks or with Bill Berrisford and Pete Bell in C1. It was still necessary to get them to do their own analysis of performance. In fact, it was even more important, because there were two paddlers in the boat, which added a new dimension to coaching. With kayaks or C1's, I could watch for times when the **crash helmet** slowed down, which was an early indication that time might be wasted at this point – as the paddler changed direction by slowing the boat. Sometimes it **might** be necessary to use a 'bow rudder' or even a reverse stroke, but if another paddler could complete the same move using forward strokes or sweep strokes, the technique needed to be examined in terms of its efficiency. With C2's I could see times when the two paddlers were actually working against each other.

Such a situation occurred with Chris Arrowsmith and Paul Brain. Chris was the smaller padder and paddled in the front. He usually had a high stroke rate and continued to exert considerable effort throughout the length of the course. Paul, in the stern, had a greater reach and tended to do most of the steering, which often meant doing a bow rudder – in which the blade is kept fixed. Turning, in this way, is effected by water acting on the stationary blade. The effectiveness of this stroke is greater when the boat is moving faster. When the boat is stationary, the stroke has no effect at all! It seemed to me that Chris was **accelerating** the boat forward fairly effectively, and Paul was **slowing** it down with similar effectiveness! Such inefficiencies are more easily seen by someone on the bank, and can be addressed by more use of video in training.

Clive Richardson and Colin Thompson had different issues to address. They seemed to be waiting for the water to 'do something' to them, and they would then react. By selecting specific places on the course, where 'attack' was more appropriate – like the exit from eddies, performance improved considerably. They had limited experience on water of this standard. It had been more a confidence issue than a matter of technique.

Alan Meikle and Colin Brown, Andy Rance and Bill Horsman and the Smith brothers had different issues to address, that were equally important. However, I was able to offer help and support where it was needed, and the squad worked well as a unit. Considering it was the first time I had been working in depth with the class at this level, the different techniques used were still based on logical and biomechanical analysis. I had had plenty of experience of this!

The structure of coaching had developed since the appointment of Hugh Mantle as National Competition Coach. Each class had its own coach during training for international events, but when the competition started, each class coach remained on a single section of the course and watched all classes on that section. In this way, the team operated as a complete unit with paddlers able to approach any coach for information on their performance.

After one coaching session, Ishbel Grant approached me close to tears. I had worked with her on previous occasions. One of the management team, not a coach, had seen her walking the course looking sufficiently 'stressed' that he approached her with the intention of helping to calm her. He had been fairly insensitive in his approach, and said "Don't worry. It's your first international and nobody is expecting too much from you. Just go out and enjoy it!" This was probably the worst thing he could have said. Ishbel interpreted his comments as implying she did not really deserve to be in the team, and that other paddlers were expected to produce results – not her. The effect on her confidence was disastrous, and she paddled well below expectation. The significant outcome of this incident was that management were expected to communicate with paddlers **through their coaches** unless it was an administrative issue that did not affect their paddling. The person concerned was equally upset at having caused the problem and, from that time onwards, was instrumental in protecting paddlers from this kind of situation.

* * * *

In the actual event, Liz Sharman won – again, and Gail Allen missed the bronze medal by less than a second. Ishbel was a full minute slower on each of her runs.

In the C2 event, Arrowsmith and Brain finished ninth, but were only six seconds off a bronze medal. The other C2's needed to find about half a minute before they were competitive. This would be the focus of winter training.

Richard Fox took the individual bronze medal, and the men's kayaks continued their dominance of the team event. Melvyn Jones with Russ Smith and Ian Raspin took gold. Andrew Gladwin, Richard Fox and Jim Jayes had to be content with fourth place. Even so, Stafford and Stone had provided three of the six men's kayaks.

* * * *

Richard Fox and Liz Sharman headed the rankings at the end of the Europa Cup,each having won one event. Meikle and Brown finished in seventh place. Good performances in the 1987 world championships were a definite possibility. Melvyn Jones and Andy Gladwin were also medal winners in Europe. Once again, Stafford and Stone Canoe club would be well represented.

* * * *

In December, 1986, the canoeing world was in shock. Paul McConkey was killed in a car accident on his way home from work, He had driven into a stationary lorry that had broken down, and was without lights on a duel carriageway outside Stone. He leaves a wife and a daughter, who was only a few months old at the time. Paul's life revolved round his family and the canoe club. He had always been an inspiration to other club members – on and off the water. Paddlers enjoyed the companionship and camaraderie he provided. It was usually Paul who repaired the isokinetic equipment in the training room or repaired floodlights. The church in Stone was packed with mourners from across the country paying their respects to a great guy. Each year, the club organises one of the Premier Division slaloms in his memory.

* * * *

In 1987, I travelled with the team to the World Championships at Bourg St Maurice as C2 coach and worked with the class in training sessions. Confidence had grown. Paddlers were now 'on the pace', and results would have been even better but for un-necessary penalties.

The system was now well established where each *class* coach took responsibility for one section of the course for official practice and for the duration of the event. I had one of the more technical sections above the main road bridge (I think it was gates 10 to 14) where the 'crunch' move was a downstream gate, on the right of the river, in an eddy below a line of rocks that jutted out from the bank. The course designer intended paddlers to break out from the main current, and reverse this gate before crossing to the left of the river. However, it is not unusual for paddlers to see an alternative approach that the course designer has overlooked. It happens **less** frequently when the course is a world championship level, because the designer should be familiar with the level of ability of those for whom the course is intended!

Competitors from several countries had noticed a small gap above this line of rocks that seemed to offer a 'quick' route to the gate. However it was crucial to hit this gap at speed, leaning backwards, so the boat would take off and 'pancake into the eddy' – a drop of about half a metre. Any tentative approach would cause the boat to stick on a flat rock above this gap and the bow would bury in the eddy. Most of the paddlers accepted this suggested route, and adopted this line of approach – except for Liz Sharman. Liz was most meticulous in her preparation. Her equipment was always in perfect condition and any scratch on the hull of her boats was treated as a personal insult by the course designer against her!

I was asking her to deliberately scrape her boat over a flat rock, at speed. Even in a world championships, this was 'unfair'. "Why should I have to damage my boat in order to negotiate the course properly?" I just told her it was faster and the decision was up to her. After more time inspecting the sequence, she accepted the incvitable.

Because I was working with the canadian paddlers for most of the time, and because I was on my particular section of gates during first runs, I did not see Liz on the last three gates of the course. However, her running time was not fast enough because she had to paddle back upstream for the pen-ultimate gate on her first run. This final sequence of three gates was upstream 28 (in an eddy on the left) followed by downstream gate 29 on the right side of the current directly opposite the upstream. Gate 30 was another downstream, but on the left of the current, making a right to left stagger (or 'off-set' – in American parlance) sequence.

It was a strenuous move, at the end of the course, to make the cross from 28, and then turn anti-clockwise **against** the current to complete 29 and 30 – **but it was faster.** The easier, and slower, alternative was to ferry glide across above gate 29 and turn **clockwise** in the eddy, using the current which would give a safe approach to the final two gates. Liz knew this and, after the earlier discussions about gate eleven, was undecided on her approach.

She came up to see me, on my section at the top of the course, and asked me what she should do! In the early years of coaching her, we had focused on her ability to plan and make decisions based on what she felt able to do safely and quickly. I had not coached her for the four years since she had won the worlds in 1983, and she was now asking **me** to make the decision for her. She did not want advice. She wanted to pass the pressure to someone else – and I was available!

I spoke to George Radford, her coach whom she later married, and told him what I had said – which was;

> "If you have any energy left to do the direct move, **without** crossing to the eddy, you have paddled too slowly from the bridge. You need to put full effort between gates 16 and 28, and then there will be no decision when you reach gate 28. You will not have enough energy to even consider the direct move!"

I told George that I had either given her the best possible advice for her second run, or had cost her all chance of a medal. I had taken the 'blame' and made the decision. I asked him to reinforce the plan without him telling Liz that he had spoken to me! It was essential that she should be free of any doubts, and that this was the **only** option. After a couple of hours, George 'reported back'. It had worked, and she was world champion – again.

* * * *

My stint as coach with the canadian doubles ended after those world championships and, once more, I needed to re-focus on my work at Stafford College. New courses were on stream and I was developing the academic side of physical education and sport. I retired from international coaching and restricted my involvement in slalom to issues of course design.

* * * *

I had started to fall out with some senior members of Stafford and Stone Canoe Club by the end of 1986, when a committee was elected in which the officers of the club seemed less concerned about the future direction of the club than I thought was appropriate. The nub of the problem was a desire on the part of the committee to continue all the club activities that were taking place at that time – but little more than that. We were running slaloms at local and national level, having social events such as barbecues, bonfires, dances and even night slaloms. I felt it was too inward looking. The course at Holme Pierrepont had opened, and would be the new national focus for slalom – and nobody seemed to share my concerns!

I continued to raise the issue at committee meetings and at events, while retaining my involvement in slalom courses and their design. Nevertheless most of my coaching was at international level. Even when working at Stone, it was usually with the international and national squad paddlers. It may have given the impression that I was not concerned about paddlers from lower echelons of the sport.

By the end of 1987, I regarded the issue of the club's future as too important an issue to remain silent – or comparatively silent – any more. An anonymous 'new' member had written an article for the club newsletter suggesting that the annual dinner and dance "seems very posh for canoeists". Liz Sharman was the guest of honour for the evening and had driven up from Suffolk for the occasion to present Richard Fox's first world championship gold medal from Jonquiere to the most promising junior paddler in the club. Even a local pub landlord was there to give the club a donation for helping out at his own fundraising events during that year.

More significantly, I thought back to the rebuttal that Ray Calverley, John MacLeod and myself had received from Manchester Canoe Club when, as world silver medal winners, we offered to paddle the Goyt slalom course, hoping to inspire some of the Novice paddlers of that time. I thought of Albert Kerr whose achievement, in winning gold medals at three consecutive world championships, went largely unrecognised by the canoeing world. Now, history was in danger of repeating itself. Liz Sharman, double world champion was presenting a world championship medal, given by a club member who had, by that time, won *six* world championship gold medals, and helped to put the club on the world map of slalom canoeing. Here we had an 'anonymous' club member saying that our main social occasion of the year was "too posh". I felt we needed to shout about the club success from the rooftops to anyone who would listen. The opportunity to promote the club was unparalleled. I was absolutely livid. In canoe slalom, clubs often regard top paddlers as 'prima-donnas', whereas, in other sports, clubs would give their back teeth to have even a *national* champion in their midst.

I submitted an article in which I espoused the aim and purpose of club social events as threefold; enjoyment for members, gratitude to family members and supporters and, thirdly, promotion of the club. Some events satisfy one purpose only. Others, such as the annual dinner and celebration of the year's achievements, satisfy *all* these aims.

The article promoted some discussion but little else.

Then, at the AGM of November 1989, I was accused by one of the club officers of being 'elitist' – as though such was a dirty word. I wrote to the club committee and, despite having being given life membership several years earlier, tended my resignation from the club.

Elitism means restricting or limiting opportunities to a few

privileged persons. I had played an integral part in the formation of the club, sixteen years earlier, specifically to help aspiring
slalomists – any aspiring slalomist! If, as seemed to be the case,
the **main** aim of the club now was for paddlers' enjoyment, I had
no role. I believed the **main** aim was to raise the standard of
performance of each and every paddler who desired it. Enjoyment
was an essential part of the individual's motivation to improve,
but was not an end in itself.

As a direct result of my letter of resignation, I was approached
by several members of the committee – including the chairman,
who pointed out that resigning from life membership would be
an insult to those who had awarded it to me. In addition, there
was far more support for my ideas than I realised. Many paddlers
had not even considered the situation, and were far more concerned with their own paddling and their own training. I needed
to step back and re-examine **my** position. Paddlers, such as Dave
Mitchell many years earlier, focused on their own situation. This
was an essential part of their success. There would be plenty of
time to get involved in the 'politics' of the sport after they had
retired. It was not that they did not care, but more that they did
not have time to care – yet! Now I had raised the issue and given
it a higher profile, there was an acceptance that the club needed
a development plan to ensure its future growth and survival.

I withdrew my letter of resignation and continued to work,
behind the scenes usually, for the development of the club.

* * * *

In 1990, Liz Sharman (in her married name of Radford) was
awarded the MBE for services to canoeing. She won eleven national
championships, two European titles and two world championships
and remains the most successful British female slalomist.

* * * *

The world championships had been held at Tacen, Jugoslavia in1955. In 1991, the site, which lies just outside Ljubljana in present-day Slovenia, was chosen again with many changes having been made to the course in the intervening years. Shaun Pearce took the gold in mens kayak and the only other medal was a bronze in the C1 team event. In that same year, in the World Cup series (five events, of which two were in the United States and three in Europe) Richard Fox took gold, and the other three mens kayaks all finished in the top ten.

* * * *

I had been retired from international involvement for almost four years when Alan Edge, the Olympic Team Coach, contacted me. Roger Mainwaring, the ladies international team coach was unable to continue in the role because of illness. The Barcelona Olympic Games were twelve months away, and Britain had not been able to 'earn' its full allocation of places for the Games.

There is a relatively complex system for Olympic selection, in which the International Olympic Committee (IOC) allocates a **total** number of competitors for each sport. For canoe slalom, there would be one hundred boats in total. The International Canoe Federation organizes its own qualification events, and chose to ensure the widest representation of countries from around the world – to promote the sport. Each country was allowed to send **one** representative boat in each class. However, **additional** places could be earned for a country by performing 'well' in those events. 1991 had not been a particularly good year for the British ladies, and the national champion of 1990 had not made the 1991 team. By the end of the year, no extra places for the ladies had been earned and we were in danger of only sending one paddler to Barcelona in this class. However, because the number of countries who wished to compete was below the permitted allocation, two additional events were to be held on the Olympic course at La Seu d'Urgell in April 1992. Good performances here could earn an extra two places for the ladies class. My role was to help in obtaining these extra places.

I had worked with Alan for almost twenty years in various roles. We understood each other's foibles, and he felt I would be able to fit into the organisation – even at this late stage. I was fully conversant with the system of 'section coaching', and understood the demands of international performance. Furthermore, I was able to obtain the necessary leave of absence from a very understanding employer – as I had done for the previous twenty years!

Throughout the winter months, I made my weekly evening trips to Nottingham, to coach the ladies squad – who, like most of the national team paddlers, had moved to this area and enrolled on higher education courses, taken employment or just 'camped' in other paddlers flats and apartments. Some of the squad had commitments away from Nottingham and definitely suffered by not being able to access the coaching on offer here.

I did not appreciate the extent to which the sport had moved on in the four years since 1987. The establishment of Holme Pierrepont as **the** centre for slalom meant that most of the top paddlers were now being coached regularly. Stone had been unique in the eighties because it was one of the few places with a floodlit slalom course. Most other paddlers were restricted to endurance and conditioning work during the week, because it was too dark to work on technique. Now, more paddlers had training grants, flexible study time, a floodlit slalom course of international standard and a supply of international coaches based in Nottingham. Their attitude was now professional. Hugh Mantle had moved the theories of the psychology of coaching to a higher plane and worked closely with Alan Edge and his team of technical coaches. The most obvious danger now was of information overload. I had focused on getting paddlers to think for themselves, make their own decisions and to be **independent**. It was a big shock to see this new environment with total support for paddlers that seemed to be creating a greater degree of **dependence** than I could accept.

I need not have worried. This new breed of slalomist, with the massive available resources they could access, was very much able to filter information and discard irrelevancies. I remember one specific occasion when I was coaching Richard Fox's sister, Rachel. I gave her the split time from my stop watch as she walked back up the course to repeat a sequence of gates – something like 38·46 seconds. Her immediate riposte was that she only wanted **tenths** of a second. Hundredths were too much to deal with when doing several timed sequences. It was not supposed to be a mental arithmetic session! I learned quickly.

Hugh Mantle had also brought Cliff Morgan, the BBC commentator, to a weekend training session at Nottingham to help paddlers deal with the press. Journalists would want information that they could use, and sought to sensationalise whenever possible – because it sold more papers! Cliff was excellent. He conducted face to face interviews with paddlers and then wrote a typical headline that might follow. He asked questions on the lines of "Have you got a chance of winning?" The resulting headline might have been – *She says she will win gold. There is a sense of arrogance in these canoeists. Many seem to be prima donnas!"* Any casual comment could be twisted in this way. Much advice was given, and much was learnt.

Several months later, when the Barcelona team had been finalised, a local journalist actually arrived to a training session at Nottingham, and asked a paddler that same question. He was probably shocked by the reply – *"If I knew who would win, it would be pointless going. Wouldn't it? Ask me another!* It showed our paddlers had entered the hard world of Olympic competition, and were becoming well prepared – on and off the water.

Hours of video recording existed for each paddler, and was used carefully. It was normally a 'one to one' review between paddler and coach. In this way the difficulties experienced by one paddler did not create problems and doubts in another paddler – where no problem previously existed.

It quickly became apparent that having the information, that a paddler might use effectively, was only important if it was requested by the paddler. The time might not be appropriate. **That** was the filter mechanism. In fact the stock question from coach to paddler on the river bank was "Do you want any information".

* * * *

During the build up to selection events, paddlers had general and specific input from the whole coaching team. I was just a cog in a well oiled machine. If all went smoothly, I would remain in the background with the other coaches, physiotherapists, psychologists, and management. If I made a mistake, it would certainly be noticed, because it would impact in other areas and would be picked up by someone else. This was not something to be concerned about. It contributed to a vibrant coaching group. Issues that arose when working with paddlers were addressed in management meetings. Action plans were devised that were designed to improve our efficiency in getting the best from paddlers.

At one 'team building' session for all the coaches and officials, we were asked to write one **positive** comment about each person in the room, on separate pieces of paper – how the person had helped them, how reliable they were or about their level of efficiency. We each received our dozen pieces of paper and were able to reflect on how we contributed to the success of the group. This was the easy part. We were then asked to write one thing we would change about the person that would improve their effectiveness. I received my pieces of paper and the main comments were – 'uses ten words when one would be sufficient', 'needs to be more precise', important detail given – but sometimes at the wrong time'. It was something I needed to address, but the supportive way the group operated meant there was no real threat. Other individuals had received equally forthright feedback. We all had our own demons to remove!

* * * *

By the time we travelled to the Olympic site in April 1992, the coaches, managers and other officials were a fully functional and integrated team. I had spent each week working with the ladies during the winter, as a part of their support. Other coaches had made their contributions.

We were able to acquire the two extra places for the ladies, and Rachel Fox, Karen Like and Lynn Simpson were selected. Two Canadian crews qualified at the fourth World Cup event of the year at Merano in June – less than two weeks before numbers had to be finalised with the British Olympic Association.

The Olympic team consisted of three mens kayaks, thr e ladies kayaks, three canadian singles, and two canadian doubles, a total of thirteen paddlers. The benefit of this was in having coaches for each class who would be able to adopt a section of the course, in the way we had done for the past few major international events. Countries that had smaller entry numbers would need to co-operate with each other in order to cover the course effectively and provide the necessary information to their paddlers.

* * * *

Olympic selection did not go completely to plan. Paddlers were far more familiar with the need to 'peak' for the main events of the year. This involves, among other things, reducing the amount of endurance and conditioning work while increasing the intensity of training and speed work. There is a limited number of times each year that a paddler can taper down before it affects performance.

Shaun Pearce had won the 1991 world championships in Tacen, and had applied for 'pre-selection' in March, which would have enabled him to continue preparation up to the Games without the need to taper down for a selection event in May. Gareth

Marriott, as the undisputed best C1 paddler in Britain, also applied. Inevitably, Richard Fox also applied, because if Shaun was pre-selected, there would only be two places left – and anything could happen in a selection event. This gave us a major headache. Richard had been world champion four times, and was at the top of the world rankings because he had won the World Cup series in 1991. Shaun was the current world champion, but only ranked ninth in the final World Cup standings, whereas Melvyn Jones was ranked fourth, and Ian Raspin tenth It was a nice problem to have – four paddlers in the top ten in the world!

It was decided that there was not enough justification to pre-select Shaun. However, although there was a *stronger* case for pre-selecting Gareth and Richard, the backlash would have been too disruptive and nobody was pre-selected. This 'failure' to act led to the resignation of Roger Annan, who had been chairman of the National Slalom Executive Committee for fourteen years. Roger had worked tirelessly in his support and backing of the Team Management group over the years, and had often defended decisions that had been opposed by rank and file members of the General Slalom Committee, many of whom believed that too many changes were being made in the interest of the national teams and against the interests of the 'average' club paddler.

In the final selection events, Shaun missed out, and Ian Raspin joined Richard Fox and Melvyn Jones in the Olympic Team.

* * * *

Most of the paddlers were able to fly to the Olympic site in the Spanish Pyrenees for one week training sessions. Others, with less financial resources available to them, joined us in the Bedford Midi mini-buses that towed large canoe trailers. By sharing the driving between three people (two hours at the wheel and then four hours rest in the back of the vehicle), the journey from Nottingham took about twenty two hours including the Channel crossing, and we arrived fresh at the end of it. For me, it was a throw back to an earlier age in the seventies when all travel was by road, and I had driven a Morris minivan from Bourg St Maurice to Calais in seventeen hours by myself – because I had failed to realise that my passenger did not have a driving licence! This was far more civilised and better organised.

* * * *

Tragedy hit the sport again in June. Martyn Hedges was killed in a road accident near Bath, less than two months before he was due to compete in the Olympic Games. He had been British Champion thirteen times since he first appeared in the world championships at Skopje in 1975, and had won medals at several events since then.

He had started paddling canadian singles after the 1972 Olympics, and would have been a major medal contender in any era of the sport. Out of respect, a decision was made **not** to send a replacement.

* * * *

John MacLeod was Olympic Team Manager, and must have experienced a mix of emotions since he competed at Munich in 1972. In everything but name, the British Team was now professional. The Olympic experience is amazing, and well documented elsewhere. Therefore, my comments are focused on the issues surrounding the slalom, and the support of paddlers in their search for optimum performance.

After the Official Opening Ceremony, and the biggest firework display I have ever seen, we made the journey back to our small satellite village in La Seu d'Urgell. Security was a major issue, and had been at all Olympic Games since the terrorist attack on Israeli competitors in Munich. Access to both the accommodation and the competition site were closely monitored, but security was at a much lower level than in Barcelona. We were able to move freely round the town which made the whole atmosphere more like a world championship. There was no major 'step-up' to Olympic level. We were in familiar territory, and the paddlers would still be competing against the best in the world. Maintaining focus would be quite straightforward. Furthermore, the only competitors in the town were canoe slalomists.

In Barcelona, the distractions were far greater. Many different sports were competing. Competitors whose events were finished were living in close proximity to those in the final days of preparation. There were those who wished to celebrate their success, and others who wanted to drown their sorrows. The food halls were open twenty four hours each day, and there was the added problem of 'celebrity spotting'. Competitors who were household names in their sport were celebrities to competitors from other sports, and posed an added distraction. It was a major bonus to be a two hour drive from the main Olympic site, and, with the added altitude in the foothills of the Pyrenees, much cooler and more pleasant.

* * * *

For the main event there was a much smaller start list as the IOC had limited the overall number of entries – and there were no team events. The starting interval between competitors was increased, so that television could cover the full run of each boat. Spectators were restricted to the right bank while the left bank was reserved for the organisers, coaches, and competitors, and gave excellent vantage points for section coaching. Separation from spectators because of safety and security issues did have its advantages!

The results reflected our high level of planning and organisation. In the Men's K1, Richard Fox came fourth, missing the bronze by a fraction of a second. Melvin Jones was seventh. Gareth Marriott took silver in the C1 event. It could easily have been gold apart from a small touch with the last few centimetres of his boat on one gate. Lynn Simpson made the top ten in the ladies. The best C2 finished twelfth. The management and coaching team had done their job.

The time slot, in which Martyn Hedges would have paddled, was maintained, and resulted in a three minute gap when nobody was on the water. Each individual had their private moments to reflect on the contribution that Martyn had made to the sport.

It had been a successful Games and John MacLeod was able to fully justify the support we had received from the BOA. This was probably the most important factor because international training grants were now allocated on the basis of international performance. Grants for 1993 were secure!

* * * *

Back at home, I had spent very little time with Stafford and Stone Canoe Club. 1992 had been a very good year for the club. It organised the Paul McConkey Memorial event at Bala, the Division One event at Holme Pierrepont and the mini-slaloms in Stone at the start of the year. It provided the course design erection and maintenance team for the World Cup event at Nottingham that several countries were using to finalise their Olympic Selection.

The real bonus for the club was that the Stone site was chosen for the National Under 14 and under 16 Championships that were held at the end of May and organised by Andy Neave. Andy had really taken to the role of coach organiser, and was working with a group of paddlers that included a fourteen year old Laura Blakeman who, through his guidance, progressed to international level, and represented Britain in the Sydney Olympic Games. Andy Roden was in the group and eventually transferred to paddling C2 with his elder brother. They have also become established international paddlers.

The whole focus of the club had shifted towards paddler development – especially junior paddlers who would eventually feed into national teams. Nottingham was a superb facility for established paddlers who could fund themselves away from their home environment, but there was no real **club** that would provide the support, or meet their needs away from the sport. There was not even a clubhouse! Stafford and Stone was now a community club with paddlers of all levels of ability and commitment. More importantly, it now had direction and ambition, that culminates each year in the National Interclub Championships in which the club continues to be successful.

At the end of the year, Donald Bean, whose altruistic donations of equipment and finance had benefited the club immensely, was awarded the MBE in the Queen's New Year's Honours List.

* * * *

I continued to work with the national team, specifically as ladies coach. The next World Championships, in 1993, would be held in the small town of Mezzana on the River Sole in northern Italy. Most of the ladies squad was based in Nottingham and I was able to continue my weekly trips there during the winter. However, it was a far more difficult task because of the greater variation in standard and level of experience of the paddlers. Those who had benefited from membership of the Olympic squad were better able to identify their own training needs. They were able to train much of the time as individuals, seeking help and information when necessary. The less experienced paddlers still wanted to know the training times of their 'rivals', even though it made no difference to how they tackled the course! Perhaps it was a confidence issue, with the less experienced paddlers feeling a greater need to know their relative standing within the group, and whether they were likely to make selection. The outcome was that there was far less co-operation between members of the squad. We had an Olympic squad and the rest. Gradually, the group were able to reach some degree of integration.

An additional issue was the return of Maria Lund, who had taken time away from the sport to have her first child. Her Husband,

Chris was one of the team physiotherapists. Maria was one of the best technicians in the squad and could perform sequences that were beyond the scope of many of the others. Unfortunately, she was more mentally fragile than the others and easily upset when stressed. She was a paddler who performed instinctively, and attempts to get her to analyse her own performance were likely to be viewed as criticism of her performance. Inevitably, I stepped back and intervened only when asked to do so – by her. It was useful having her husband as team physiotherapist because it gave me an extra channel of communication!

* * * *

Selection took place at the beginning of May, with two events on the same weekend at Grandtully. Shaun Pearce, as the defending world champion, was pre-selected to allow him to defend his title. Richard Fox and Melvyn Jones joined him, with Ian Raspin as fourth man. Ian's brother, Andy, was selected to replace Richard for those international events that followed the world championships – because he had stated his intention to retire after the championships. The first **non-selected** paddler, who just missed out, was Dave Crosbee, who had married Rachel Fox at the end of 1992, and I was concerned that this might have had an affect on her. My fears were groundless. Her 'professional' approach was brilliant, with Dave giving full support.

The top three ladies were Rachel, Lynn Simpson and Maria Francis. Heather Corrie was the fourth boat and would not compete in the team event. Maria was the only one of the four who was not based in Nottingham and this made training for the team event difficult. It was not dissimilar to the situation thirty years earlier, where Ray Calverley, John MacLeod and myself were not selected for the team event because Dave Mitchell was the number one paddler. The difference was that Heather was quite willing to participate in team event training in Maria's place, while we experimented with paddling order. In addition, there was now far more squad training, where issues such as this could be resolved.

* * * *

Once again, the team coaching was effective, and class coaches were assigned a section of the course from which to extrapolate any information that might be useful to paddlers – safest routes, fastest lines, paddlers worth watching, and so on.

In the actual event Richard won his fifth individual gold medal, with Melvyn Jones and Shaun Pearce in third and fourth places. The same three paddlers took gold in the team event. Lynn Simpson came fifth with Rachel and Maria having too many penalties. However, in the team event the ladies won the bronze medal, which had seemed unlikely after the individual runs had been completed. Each of the canadian singles paddlers had minor disasters on their individuals runs, but came together well to take silver in the team event.

It had been another good event, in which Britain won five medals.

* * * *

Richard had won individual gold and team gold. His French wife Myriam had won the ladies individual gold at the same championships.

The Mezzana world championships were the end of an era. Until Richard Fox came on the scene, no kayak paddler had won the world title more than twice. Richard was retiring from competition with five individual world championship gold medals, five team gold medals and an individual bronze. He had World Cup titles and European titles as well. Furthermore, he had been an inspiration to a whole nation of paddlers who would now take the sport forward.

* * * *

The 1995 World Championships were scheduled for Nottingham. Once again, as the only available member of the coaching team who was also an International Judge, I would be the British member of the Course Design Commission. It was considered unnecessary to resign from coaching duties because there were now sufficient safeguards in place to prevent 'inside' information being given to paddlers from the host country. This was much different to the situation that existed in 1981. Sufficient video coverage of paddlers meant that everything was much more open. Each country videoed its own paddlers *and* any other paddler whose technique or strategy on a gate sequence might give them useful information.

I retained the duel roles of ladies class coach and course design commissioner. The other members of the course commission would not be known until the start of 1995, which meant I could focus on my coaching role. Alan Edge, as the head coach, gave me a free hand in designing courses at training weekends, selection events and major slaloms that were organised by the National Slalom Committee – like the British Open event at the end of each year. I put together *another* file of possible moves and sequences that could be used in course design. I was looking for sequences that would test each of the classes. Frequently, I came across sequences that were very difficult for C2's, with their increased width and length, but which were straightforward for the kayaks, who remained relatively unchallenged. It was essential to avoid a situation where success depended more on speed, strength and endurance than on the skill of the paddler. Safe slower options had to be available when more difficult, risky and quicker moves were offered. If these safe options did not exist, team managers would not approve the course prior to the event, and *they* would dictate how the course would be changed *in order to make it possible* – which was limit of their 'rights'. From my point of view, it was an academic challenge to produce a course that would be as difficult as possible for the best paddlers in the world, **but** gave an easier and slower alternative to paddlers who lacked the skills to compete effectively at this level. It was a game of chess – course designer versus slalom competitor.

* * * *

Events went pretty much as expected in 1994. Britain's position as a major slalom nation was assured. Shaun Pearce (K1M), Lynn Simpson (K1L) and Gareth Marriott (C1) each topped the Final World Rankings in their own class. We could look forward with confidence to the world championships on our own course in the following year.

There was one final twist to the end of year celebrations. Twenty one years since its foundation, the committee of Stafford and Stone Canoe Club decided to hold an anniversary dinner on 4th November, 1994, to celebrate its achievements. The opportunity existed to promote and publicise the club's achievements and officially mark Richard Fox's retirement. Chairman, Dave Royle and a subcommittee of members, including myself, organised the event and a photographic exhibition of club activities. High profile performers from the sport and local community were invited to attend. Melvin Jones from the club, seventh in the 1992 Olympics, was invited with his German wife Lisa, who was the reigning Olympic Champion from Barcelona. Richard Fox and his wife Myriam were invited – both as current world champions. Joan Holland, the Mayor of Stone also attended. All five were guests of honour at the dinner attended by more than a hundred people. The mayor paid tribute to the achievements of the club and to Richard and Melvyn and their respective wives. The event achieved good coverage in the local press and in canoeing journals. We, as the sub-committee organising the event, thought it had been a great success and a fitting tribute. Unfortunately, at least one member of the club committee resigned and we lost a few members because they were vehemently opposed to paying for the 'guests of honour' from club funds.

We seemed to have been here before! Publicity is the lifeblood of an organisation. Success breeds success. It is not rocket science to recognise the need to publicise achievements. Ask any major advertising company why they sponsor sport. Firstly, their product reaches a wider audience. Secondly, people **want** to be associated with success. Why do schools have prize giving evenings? Why do universities have degree ceremonies?

We had to accept that each person is entitled to their own opinion, and that those who disagreed with the policy and direction of the club were out of step with the majority of members. Membership had never been compulsory!

* * * *

Selection for the 1995 World Championships took place at Holme Pierrepont. Although this was the obvious choice of venue, it was a surprise to some people that selection was delayed until the beginning of May. However, the world championships were scheduled for the last week of August, and the first of four World Cup events was not until the end of June. This gave plenty of time to arrange travel and accommodation.

There were several squad weekends at Nottingham to bring paddlers together, and familiarise new team members with the tried and tested system that had to be regularly 'tweaked' for each course on which we competed. Easter Grandtully was the **third** Premier Division event of the season, and competition weekends were complemented with separate training camps for the various classes.

Then, on April 22nd, we travelled to the 'inaugural' international slalom and Pan-Celtic Cup event, held on the newly completed Teesside White Water Course at Stockton on Tees. The event was advertised in the ICF calendar, although the majority of paddlers were from the 'home' nations plus the French National Team who were combining the event with training sessions at Nottingham in preparation for the World Championships later in the year.

The weather was fine and sunny, the river was a good test of slalom ability, but a strong breeze blew off the sea and caused **major** problems with the slalom gates. There was a serious design fault that had not been picked up at the planning stage. In all major national and international competitions for the preceding twenty years, **one** gate was suspended from each bearer wire; otherwise a touch on one gate would cause any other gates on that wire to move. One of the best systems in the world had been designed by John MacLeod and had proved to be effective on Holme Pierrepont – which was much wider than Teesside, but equally susceptible to windy conditions. The main feature of the Nottingham system was that the main bearer wire could be put under extreme tension, which prevented any noticeable 'swing' effect that would occur if the wire was slack. The Teesside system had been designed and tested in a large indoor warehouse, and consisted of a latticework of interconnected cables suspended over the course. Gates were suspended from this latticework. Parts of this lattice were three or four metres above the level of the water. Hitting one gate caused movement in several others that were upstream or downstream of it. Once in motion, it could take twenty or thirty seconds for a gate to stop swinging. With the added factor of a strong breeze, penalties on gates became a lottery.

It was 'our' most recent artificial course, and we were morally bound to remain at the site for the weekend. Teesside Development Corporation had invested a lot of time and money on the project. The French, never slow to make their feelings known, packed up at the end of the first day, and travelled down to Nottingham for more productive training sessions.

Shortly after this incident, Alan Edge and I were asked to provide a written report on the suitability of the site for national and international competition. Our report compared Teesside with Nottingham, and recommended immediate changes to the system of suspending slalom gates on the Teesside course. I was also concerned about the **safety** side. Nottingham has a thirty

centimetre wall, down both sides of the course between the pe-
destrian walkway and the river, into which three or four metre
steel poles can be anchored. The wall is a 'natural' barrier that
keeps people with prams and pushchairs from straying too close
to the water. There is no such barrier at Teesside, and I witnessed
the frightening site of a pushchair, complete with frightened tod-
dler, rolling down the path towards the water, with the anxious
parent shouting to anyone who would listen to "stop the pram!".
There was **no** safety wall at Teesside. As far as I am aware, no
action was taken to correct this design flaw. I have not been there
since.

* * * *

Two weeks later, World Cup and World Championship selection
took place at Nottingham over the three days of the bank holiday
weekend at the beginning of May. The final event in the World
Cup series had the added importance of being on the River Ocoee
in Tennessee, which would host the canoe slalom event for the
1996 Olympic Games.

Once again, it was Stafford and Stone Canoe Club that
erected the selection event course I had designed, and which
had been approved by Alan Edge as National Team Coach. They
would also be erecting and maintaining the course for the World
Championships, and this was good practice for them.

As expected, the team consisted mainly of those who lived
and trained at Nottingham. This was a good sign, and showed
that time training on this site would be of great benefit in the
forthcoming world championships. However, it did sound warn-
ing bells for me. Some paddlers were spending nearly all of their
'water time' on Nottingham. I thought back to the days when
the South of England paddlers did most of their training on the
Thames weirs and mastered the 'boils and eddies' far better than
most of the Northern paddlers; **but** they lost the ability to 'read'
water patterns on the more natural rivers, or to choose the best

route between submerged rocks on sites that were unfamiliar to them. It seemed to me that some paddlers had never experienced 'tripping over' a paddle and were unaccustomed to choosing optimum lines down a course. This was not a serious problem for the **elite** paddlers, but not all paddlers at Nottingham were in this category.

* * * *

Commitments at work, the 'day job', prevented me from going to the first three World Cup events, but I flew out a few days before the Mezzana event with other team members. We landed in Munich, and were met by Dave Crosbee in one of the team hired vehicles, and then continued by road over the Brenner Pass into Italy. I was experiencing pain in my left leg, which became progressively more severe and swollen during the next couple of days. When Jane Wilson, the team doctor, saw it, I was promptly whisked away to the local doctor with a suspected thrombosis – possibly caused by the flight from England. This was a new experience for me, and I did not appreciate its seriousness at the time. I was driven by a local Italian ambulance driver to the main hospital in Trento – which was an even more frightening experience. It was downhill all the way and the ambulance driver was probably an experienced or aspiring rally driver in his spare time. With blue flashing light and siren blaring, it was just like being in England, judging by the amount of time spent on the wrong side of the road. When we reached the Autostrada, he sped on down the valley, but we encountered a traffic hold up outside Trento. This caused no significant problems, because he just continued on the hard shoulder and, when this was blocked by stationary traffic, we did several hundred yards on the grass verge at the side of the road!

I spent three days in hospital, on antibiotics and undergoing various tests and treatments until the swelling finally disappeared. The team transport came down from Mezzana and collected me for a much more sedate return journey to the site. Arriving just before the individual runs were due to start, I remained a spectator as Gareth Marriott and Lynn Simpson took golds in their respective events. Then, fully recovered, we set off by road for the following week's World Cup event at Lofer, on the River Saalach in Austria.

* * * *

Lofer is a small town close to the city of Salzburg. Today it is the site of the British Olympic Assocation's training venue for a variety of sports including bob-sleigh, skiing, and athlete conditioning facilities for a host of Olympic and non-Olympic sports. In 1995, things were different. The organisers catered well for the spectators and visitors to the town – which is in an area noted for tourism. Unfortunately, canoe slalom in Austria had not moved on from its glory days of the sixties and seventies. Kurt Presslmayr, who had taken twelve medals in slalom and white water racing world championships, during that era, including winning both the slalom **and** the white water race at Spittal in 1965, had long since gone. Norbert Sattler, the Olympic silver medallist in Munich and the 1973 world champion, had retired too. The whole aura of this event was that of an organisation lacking in vitality and needing rejuvenation.

I particularly noticed the course, which lacked imagination in its design and seemed to depend more on the ease of access to trees on the river bank than to obvious features and wave patterns on the water. Small matters of detail, such as the angle of the bearer wire to the current flow, seemed to have been ignored. Judges were positioned in places where it was difficult to see whether negotiation of the gate was completed correctly and whether the boat had crossed the gateline. We had managed to get an **extra** judge allocated to one section because of one such situation. Adding to the organisers problems, there was the issue of variable water level throughout the event on this river, that was

176

fed by natural and uncontrolled 'run-off' from the surrounding hills. I detected a lack of enthusiasm among the paddlers that was only offset by the realisation that this really was a World Cup event!

A more significant memory for me, than the whole of the Lofer event, was a discussion I had with Stuart McIntosh, one of the C1 paddlers. Stuart was a very strong minded and determined paddler who had qualified for the team by training **outside** the national squad. His natural ability was obvious, but he was reluctant to accept help from myself or other coaches – perhaps because he regarded 'outside' help as criticism or as a threat to his independence. In retrospect, he was probably right to continue to operate *for this event* using the strategy and approach that had got him there in the first place. The time to begin working with paddlers is at home, in a non-threatening environment, building up a relationship where mutual trust exists. Stuart took very little information from coaches – not even the available split times on each section, because he had no experience of making use of the information. We talked for some time, and I suspect I learned more from the conversation than he did! It is so important to take the time to reflect. However, I did manage to convince him to put something on his feet while walking up and down the course! There always seemed to be paddlers who, because they wore nothing on their feet while in the boat, insisted on walking around in bare feet. Stuart was one of these paddlers. I failed to see the logic in jeopardising one's chances in an event because of a gashed foot from a piece of jagged rock.

All events are memorable in some way. At this event, possibly because I had been taken ill in Mezzana, I felt very underused by paddlers. They took information on the various section splits, but I felt I had far more information to give on the best lines between gates, the angle of the boat to the current, and on where time was being lost in comparison to boats from other teams. Consequently, I did not feel confident in our chances by the time competition began.

In the heats, Stuart McIntosh and Craig Brown made the final fifteen in C1. Lynn Simpson (K1L), and Andy Raspin (K1M) were the only other paddlers to qualify for their respective finals, with Lynn finishing with the silver medal. It was not a good competition. Fortunately, the forthcoming world championships were being held on our own course – which was much more familiar territory.

* * * *

Back in Stone, the National Rivers Authority had just completed refurbishment work on the river and its surrounds. On previous occasions, we had been able to influence their designs to underpin the supports of the historic Medieval bridge that spans the river in a series of three arches at this point. The Authority had intended to put stone supports round the base of the bridge to prevent further erosion, but they also planned to channel the river flow **equally** through all three arches. Through discussion and negotiation, we had persuaded them to channel more water through the centre arch, which was much better for slalom canoeing. It sounded quite simple, but, quite often, simple solutions are not forthcoming when related to the preservation of 'ancient monuments'. I do not know whether the ease with which discussions had taken place, concerning the bridge preservation, influenced these later discussions, but the club had now been fully consulted in plans by the NRA to upgrade the club's training site. Finance was provided from several 'pots' of money – navigation, recreation, conservation, flood prevention and fishing (because our alterations to the bed of the river created turbulence that aerated the water and provided increased oxygen!). New paths were laid. The river banks were further reinforced to prevent erosion. Steel posts were fixed along both banks of the river. Hedges were layered, and the car park was resurfaced.

Dave Royle, the club chairman, joined the Mayor of Stone and an official from the NRA, and presided at a 'ribbon cutting' ceremony at the club's annual Fourth and Novice Divisions' slalom in July, 1995. Once again, the importance of maintaining links within the local community had been effective. The status of the club had been further enhanced and recognised as a significant organisation in the regional provision for sport and recreation.

* * * *

Training continued on Holme Pierrepont when we returned from Lofer, and I spent time producing a course plan, as I had done for Bala fourteen years earlier. All the post holes (for the three and four metre poles from which gate bearer wires would be suspended) were marked on the plan – as well as the predominant wave patterns, stoppers, eddies and direction of flow of the water throughout the length of the course.

In this way, all visiting teams could work from the same overall plan and, when it was designed and published, all teams would have their copy of the final course superimposed on this plan. It was essential, for the credibility of the organisers, that everything was 'above board' **and** seen to be above board.

The World Championships were the largest canoeing event that had been held in Britain. Since 1981, when the Championships were in Bala, new countries had entered the world stage. Croatia, Slovenia and Bosnia Herzegovina had their own teams that replaced the former Yugoslavia. Similarly, Latvia, Russia, Czech Republic, Slovakia and the Ukraine replaced the Soviet bloc. Countries from Africa and South America added to the numbers so that over thirty nations were represented. With a maximum of four paddlers from each country, in each event, there were over a hundred entries for the men's kayak singles event, of who one third would progress to the Sunday finals.

The River Trent was disappointingly low, even for the time of year. The course would need to be even more technical to make up for the lack of power in the water, but this is never a problem at Nottingham. It is still one of the best artificial courses in the canoeing world – considering that there is only a two metre drop in its four hundred metre length.

I met the other members of the Course Design Commission. Tibor Sykora, who I worked with at Bala was still involved, and had travelled the world to successive championships. It was good to see him again. We watched paddlers perform sequences with varying degrees of success and I was, once again, able to produce a variety of options for each section – with a comparable sequence at a different part of the course, so there would be no bias in favour of left or right handed canadian paddlers. This was not an issue for C1's who could 'switch', as some of the successful American paddlers had done at Jonquiere and Bala. The offset cockpits of the C2 made 'switching' more difficult and left / right bias needed to be considered. I did not need to be part of the final decision -making process because neither Tibor nor I wanted an 'easy', or straightforward, course. There had to be fast 'risky' options that could be chosen against the slower safe option. Different competition classes would favour different options and it would be a serious test of skill for all.

We submitted the course to the organising committee. I had some concerns about the final sequence, especially the penultimate gate which was upstream on the back of a stopper, because there was no safe and slow option to this 'risky move. The rest of the course was a difficult and fair challenge, but one gate took greater significance than any other on the course. I had always focused on sustained difficulty throughout the **whole** of the course, but, on this occasion, I was outvoted.

Once again, the course was approved at the Team Managers' Meeting – without change, and we were ready to begin. It was a source of pride for me to see Stafford and Stone Canoe Club face the challenge of getting the course erected. The course was in position in a couple of hours – much quicker than had occurred in Lofer a few weeks earlier – or anywhere else for that matter! All spare wires, gates and loose pieces of terylene gate adjusters were removed and stored. This club would win any competition in course erection. Furthermore, it was a matter of pride. Dave Royle, the club Chairman had said as much in his exhortation for help with the course at the Paul McConkey Memorial event in June. "If we get this one right, we'll have the **privilege** of erecting and maintaining the course at the World Championships." Several officials from other nations commented on the efficiency and almost 'military' precision, and it was taken as a personal insult if someone said a gate **might** need adjusting.

* * * *

After practice runs, the first qualifying events took place on Wednesday, 30th August. Gareth Marriott was the only C1 to progress to the finals. In the ladies' event, Heather Corrie Qualified comfortably, but Rachel Crosbee and Lynn Sin.pson, the number one ranked lady in the world, had nervous waits before eventually progressing in fifteenth and sixteenth place out of the seventeen qualifiers. Neither of the C2's qualified. On the Thursday, all four mens' kayaks went through – with Ian Raspin heading the list of qualifiers. The coaches had a great deal of work in front of them before the Finals Days.

Class coaches still operated the same system of 'bank support' for the competition, but I was not allocated a section of the course because of my duties with the Course Design Commission. This gave me more freedom to cover the whole course. British paddlers, especially those based in Nottingham, tended to consult widely with those coaches who had been involved in their training. For many paddlers, this might be two or three different coaches. I had worked closely with three of the ladies, but not with Kath Pigdon because she was unable to travel to Nottingham on a regular basis. The requests for information varied. The ladies usually wanted very specific information on one or two gates, or, maybe, the split time of a named paddler on one particular section. Too much information, especially if it conflicted with **their** own analysis, would undermine confidence. The men's kayaks seldom lacked confidence and were more likely to ask "Is there anything I need to know?" They had a greater ability to filter information, and could reject anything that was inappropriate to their plans. It was still important for **me** to select **my** comments carefully!

In the Ladies Team event, Britain was in gold medal position after first runs with just one penalty, but, on second runs, the French team went clear and were only a fraction of a second outside the British time. This gave the gold medal to the French team, and Britain had to be content with the silver. The C1 team was well outside the medals, having picked up too many penalties on the lower part of the course.

On the Friday, it was the turn of the canadian singles. Gareth Marriott was number one in world rankings for 1994, and the favourite for the gold. It was his 'home' competition water and also his training site. His fifteenth place was disappointing for himself and for the many supporters who cheered him down the course, but he was only **seven** seconds behind the winner, Davy Hearn from the USA. The margin of error in slalom is very small! Some consolation was provided, on the same day, by the K1 men who took the bronze medal in the team event – behind Germany and Slovenia.

We had no representatives in the C2 finals but the Ladies finals were on the same day. Heather Corrie was given a fifty second penalty for missing a gate and was last of the seventeen finalists at the end of first runs. A nervous and tentative Lynn Simpson was second down the course because of her low qualifying position. Too many penalties put her in tenth place, but Rachel Crosbee was lying in gold medal position after first runs – as she had been after first runs in the team event.

Lynn spent time discussing her tactics with Alan Edge before her second run, as she had done hundreds of times before on this site. She posted a clear round that was a second and a half faster than any of the first run competitors and three seconds better than Rachel. She had to wait for the rest of the paddlers to complete their runs. Heather Corrie improved but not enough to threaten Lynn's time. Streipecke from Germany went eleven hundredths of a second faster than Rachel, then Anne Boixel of France also beat Rachel's time, pushing her out of the medals.

Lynn was guaranteed a medal but the colour depended on the last two paddlers – both from the Czech Republic.

Both Czech paddlers missed the penultimate gate on the course, which equates to a fifty second time penalty. This was the gate I had been most concerned about at the design stage. It was a sad day for those two paddlers, but I felt no sadness! Lynn Simpson was world champion and Rachel Crosbee was in a very creditable fourth place.

The last day, Sunday, was the final of the individual men's kayaks. It was the first time since 1975 that Richard Fox was not competing in a world championship. There was no particular favourite. Several paddlers, including Ian Raspin, the top qualifier, were potential medallists.

Paul Ratcliffe, in fifth place, finished best of the British paddlers. The gold medal went to Oliver Fix of Germany. It was a tremendous celebration for the German team who produced a banner with the word 'FOX', in which they had crossed out the 'O' and replaced it with 'I'. It was a fitting tribute by them to Richard Fox. Oliver Fix had taken his crown.

* * * *

At the World Cup Finals, on the Ocoee river in September, Gareth Marriott and Lynn Simpson won their respective events, and finished the year at the top of the World Cup rankings. Kath Pigdon, who under-performed at the world championships did win the Junior Pre-World championships. Shaun Pearce was placed third in the World rankings. The future looked very bright.

* * * *

As the number of countries interested in slalom canoeing increased, it became progressively more difficult to qualify for Olympic Games. Places for the one hundred and twenty boats, that were allocated to the ICF by the Atlanta Organising Committee, were contested by the various nations during 1995. Britain had qualified four men's kayaks, one Canadian single's paddler, and two ladies kayaks. In the early season selection events, these places had been allocated to Ian Raspin, Shaun Pearce, Andy Raspin and Paul Ratcliffe in men's kayak, Lynn Simpson and Rachel Crosbee in Ladies kayak, and Gareth Marriott in Canadian singles. The Olympic committees of several countries had decided not to send their full complement of slalomists, preferring to send competitors in other sports. This meant that there were extra places 'up for grabs' at the first World Cup event in April 1996 – on the Olympic course. Mark Delaney, with an excellent eighth place, qualified in C1, and Craig Brown and Stuart Pitt qualified in C2. We now had a team of ten paddlers, which allowed us to take additional coaching staff, which meant we could cover the whole course in sections of four or five gates. With a physiotherapist, psychologists, and Brian Fuller as team manager, we were as well equipped as any other team apart from the USA.

* * * *

At regular intervals, we had travelled as a squad to Atlanta for one week training camps. These trips were essential to understand the issues of acclimatisation and the management of 'jet lag' as we crossed the various time zones on the eight hour flight across the Atlantic. Each camp was an opportunity to refine the system that would benefit paddlers in their preparation. Location of video playback facilities, standardisation of data presentation and transport to and from the competition site were additional factors to consider, and there were the individual needs of each paddler. Lynn, for example, wanted to do regular flat water sessions – as she did in the UK. **One,** of many situations we were able to provide, was an early morning session on a set of flat water training gates suspended over a small pool close to the training camp – where she could train on her own. One of the coaches would drive her to this site before breakfast, and spend most of the session as an observer. Actively coaching paddlers, on each occasion they trained, was not necessary. A vital part of success in international competition is being able to recreate many of the situations with which the paddler has been successful in their 'home environment. This situation gave Lynn the opportunity to assess how she was feeling, how tired she was, and how comfortable she felt in her preparation.

* * * *

The early season World Cup events took place at La Seu d'Urgell where Lynn took another gold medal, and Augsburg. There was also a 'Pre-Olympic Trial race, that the French organised at Bourg St Maurice – which was a river that had the width and force of the Olympic course, on which the paddlers would need to demonstrate their skills in a few months. The whole Olympic team, except Ian Raspin, competed. The ladies event was once again won by Lynn Simpson. Paul Ratcliffe and Andy Raspin were second and fourth in men's kayak. Gareth Marriott, in C1 had the fastest time, but one touch left him in fifth position. Nevertheless, this event produced good performances and was excellent preparation five weeks before the Olympics.

I was unable to go to any of these events. I still had my teaching at Stafford College, and needed to be careful not to impose too much on the staff, who supported me and covered my work load during extended periods of leave. The college could not have been more supportive, and paid for each period of absence in the build up to the Games. However, it was becoming increasingly more difficult to balance my teaching commitments with the increasing demands of coaching at international level.

* * * *

The Olympic Games slalom events were scheduled for Saturday, 27th July, and Sunday, 28th July, in Tennessee. The Opening ceremony took place in the city of Atlanta on the previous weekend. Then, in a fleet of hired vehicles we travelled back to our satellite village – three hours drive north from Atlanta. The atmosphere in the village was similar to our previous Olympic experience in La Seu d'Urgell. The competitors and officials were all slalom canoeists, and their various coaches and officials. Once again, it was more like a World Championship than an event in the Olympic Games. The major difference was in the increased security, and in the number of spectators who lined the banks in grandstands that extended the full length of the course. Minor differences included the insistence that paddlers, coaches and officials should only wear clothing with logos and badges of the Official team sponsors. Even personal drinks containers were subject to scrutiny. It would be unfortunate if an Olympic competitor was filmed carrying a drink that promoted the product of a firm that was not sponsoring an official team or the main Olympic event!

We had our own 'local' opening ceremony for the benefit of the community that had welcomed us unreservedly in the months leading up to the event. Then it was time for the official practice runs. All went smoothly.

Dave Mitchell, who had emigrated to the USA and developed his paddle making business with his American born wife, Peggy, was on the Course Design Commission. He had the task of designing a course that, in addition to being a fair test of paddlers at this level, was sympathetic to the demands of television, and the rest of the media. For example, any sequence that allowed a competitor to paddle back, to re-negotiate a gate or sequence, was unacceptable. It could cause confusion for many spectators 'uneducated' in slalom paddling. More importantly, it could interfere with the run of the next paddler down the course. The course needed to be fast and technically difficult. The majority of our paddlers were more than happy with the course, although there was a feeling that the needs of the media had prevented the inclusion of some 'moves' that would allow the better paddlers to demonstrate their skills. Gareth Marriott, for example, was one of the best 'technical' paddlers, and achieved success as much by his ability to make use of the water and wave patterns – positioning his boat to gain maximum advantage. A comparison might be made between his style of paddling and the Hawaiian surfers who use skill and the force of gravity to 'ride' some of the more extreme waves. **Fighting** the force of the water is not an option. Paddlers on **this** course would be tested more on strength, speed and endurance. The ability to 'use' the water would be tested – but to a lesser extent than on many other courses.

The World Cup event, held on the course in April had been won by Paul Ratcliffe in a time of 157·12 seconds. Practice times suggested that this event would be fifteen seconds quicker.

* * * *

In the ladies event, on the Saturday, Rachel Crosbee posted the third fastest time, but penalties throughout the length of the course left her out of contention. Lynn Simpson had a disastrous first run, missing several gates at the end of the course. It all now depended on second runs. Rachel could not improve on her first run, and British hopes rested with Lynn, who was the penultimate boat down the course. Her time of 161·71 was easily the fastest of the day and it looked like the gold medal run. However, one of our coaches had seen a judge signal a penalty but had not seen Lynn touch any pole. When her result came on the screen it showed a fifty second penalty for 'missing' a gate. Despite official protests, and our own inconclusive video evidence (because of the angle from which we were filming), the penalty remained. Lynn was deemed to have not properly cleared an upstream gate on the top part of the course. One disputed penalty had deprived her of a certain gold medal.

C1's also competed on the Saturday, and at the end of first runs Gareth was in the bronze medal position. It remained this way until Michal Martican, of Slovakia, among the last boats down the course, took the gold medal on his second run and pushed Gareth into fourth place. Mark Delaney, with penalties on each run, finished fourteenth.

On the Sunday, in the C2 event, Stuart Pitt and Colin Brown finished in twelfth place – which was a fair reflection of their world ranking, and then it was the turn of the men's kayaks. Ian Raspin was in fourth place after first runs with a clear run, and less than five seconds behind the leader. He did not improve on his second run and finished in ninth place, with Paul Ratcliffe 14th, and Shaun Pearce in 25th place.

The Atlanta Olympic Games is a story of what **might** have been. However, paddlers from every other country would have similar stories! The margins that determine success in international competition are infinitely small. The only consistent factor is the overall quality of the paddling which was supremely high. It was time to move on!

* * * *

On returning home, I decided that it was now time to **really** retire from international coaching. The changes that had occurred in the sport over the years that I had been involved, meant that coaching at this level could only be a full time position. It was too late for me. I returned to my teaching post at Stafford College, continuing with slalom coaching, course design and competition at local and national level. Sport and physical education was a much more 'academic' subject than when I first started teaching in 1970. Exercise physiology, sport psychology and biomechanics were far more significant. They were recognised as major determinants of success in sport. I had been in a privileged position, that allowed me to apply these principles to slalomists over the years that the sport was in its infancy. Now, slalom had matured, and British paddlers were able to perform with distinction on the world stage.

* * * *

Working in the college was always satisfying. Seeing the improvement made by individual students, as they matured and progressed into employment and higher education, was rewarding. However, it was not enough. I had spent thirty years as a **performance** coach, and the role differed in emphasis from the true physical education teacher, whose function was to educate and develop individuals **through** participation in sport and physical activity. The different sports in school are usually compulsory activities. It matters little whether the sport is rugby, basketball or football, because the skills developed are generic, and include, health, fitness, leadership and social skills. Did not a well known educationalist suggest that "The Battle of Waterloo was won on the playing fields of Eton"?

Retirement from international coaching, and performance coaching, left a minor vacuum in my life, but this did not last long! By October, 1996, I was an accredited Staff Tutor with the National Coaching Foundation (NCF), delivering courses to coaches in **all** sports – from clay pigeon shooting to rugby league, and from orienteering to swimming. There was, and still is, a great demand for coaches who are able to improve performance in an efficient way. In many sports, coaches are working with performers whose training grants depend on success. In addition, more attention is paid to issues of child protection, disability and equity in sport, and coaches need to attend courses so that their club can access the various grants that are available for sports club development. The name of the organisation has changed from NCF to 'Sportscoach UK', but its role remains largely the same.

I was working at the college as a lecturer in physical education and sports science, but delivering courses to club coaches several times each week as well. Having retired from education, my work with Sportscoach UK has increased and now extends over a greater geographical area.

* * * *

It is now 2006. I can reflect on the growth and development of British slalom canoeing, and feel that I played my part. It was the editor of the Stafford and Stone Canoe Club Newsletter who asked me to write a few words *for the next issue* in November, 2005. It was hoped that lessons might be learned, and that we might be able to explain how the club had developed into the most successful British club in the history of the sport.

Sorry! I got carried away.

A quote, attributed to the author H.G. Wells, says – "The one thing we can learn from history is that we don't learn anything from history!" He was right. As I traced my own involvement in slalom, it became increasingly apparent that the direction of the sport resulted more from geographical accidents – chance meetings, where the actions of one individual have influenced or inspired other people. It is not possible to recreate situations that were effective in previous eras. Looking backwards gives only memories which, though pleasant in themselves, takes us no further forward. Being on the right track is not sufficient. If we are stationary, we will probably be run over by the train coming up behind us! Maybe *that* is the most important lesson!

Looking forward is much more interesting. The challenge of more nations taking up the sport, especially as the Beijing Olympics introduces slalom to millions more people, is a daunting prospect. However, expansion is only desirable if the sport is in a healthy state.

The success of Stafford and Stone Canoe Club shows that it is not sufficient to focus on those at the top of the sport. The strength in depth that enables the club to be consistently successful year on year should be a model for slalom as a whole.

* * * *

Changes have been significant in canoe slalom over the years that I have been involved. Some of these changes were planned; the majority were not! Changes have usually been effected to correct some identified problem or anomaly. For example, team event competition now takes place **after** individual runs because, in the past, those who did not enter a team event lost the benefit of practice for their individual run (that **followed** the team event). The rule change corrected this anomaly, but it had the unexpected adverse effect of reducing the status of the team event. Many paddlers give little attention to team events and some do not even enter!

A more pertinent example arose during the seventies in response to the 'new' Lettmann 'Perfekt' slalom kayak – which had been designed in response to rule changes that had removed all regulations relating to concave cross sections, and allowed designers to produce a boat of 'any shape' but meeting regulations that specified only the minimum length of 400cm and minimum width of 60 cms. The BCU and ICF decided that this boat was too dangerous to allow unrestricted slalom practice – which had been the norm for many years. The BCU Slalom Committee, on health and safety grounds, limited practice to 'official runs'. Unfortunately, many paddlers, especially in the lower divisions, were upset at the prospect of traveling many miles to a slalom with the probability of less than fifteen minutes 'water time'. Inevitably, the numbers participating in slalom started to fall, although the reasons are much more complicated and complex to be attributed to one rule change.

The fact remains that most changes have been forced upon the sport in response to situations that demanded action for reasons of fairness, health and safety, or because a simply majority vote at a Slalom Committee AGM demanded it!

I have said on numerous occasions that "All slalom training is remedial". This means that the focus in training is to correct faults in technique, to address deficiencies in strength, speed and endurance, to develop the mental toughness required in competition and to improve levels of self motivation. There are other facets that could be considered of equal importance, but they all share the same characteristic – which is that there is no correct or defined quantity for any one of them. In the competition situation, deficiencies are identified, that have adversely affected performance. For this reason slalom coaching is remedial. It is about dealing with deficiencies. The goal remains the same for performer and coach. The coach aims to develop an optimum level of performance for his paddlers. The level will depend on natural ability, available time to train and the necessary finance. It also depends on other commitments and priorities that an individual will have. Above all, the coach needs to understand the goals that the paddler has, and may have some involvement in the goal-setting process.

* * * *

Competitive sport is an artificially created concept. Its purpose is to compare performance between individuals who **choose** to compete against each other. It was not always thus. Gladiatorial contests, in Ancient Rome, offered very little choice to those who were sent into the amphitheatre for the entertainment of the baying crowds. In medieval Britain and France, duels with sword or pistol often ended in death. Even the bare-knuckle fighters at the end of the nineteenth century were often fighting to survive. 'Realism' has disappeared from many sports in the interests of health and safety. Fencers are protected with masks. Boxers wear gloves to reduce the amount of damage inflicted on an opponent. Clay pigeon shooting has grown as a sport which is a long way from the idea of hunting for food. In canoe slalom, the 'real' obstacles of rocks and overhanging trees have been replaced by slalom poles that test skill in a safe environment.

Rules and regulations in sport have been developed and refined to make comparison between performers much easier. The 'best' runner, in athletics, is the one who runs a predetermined distance at a predetermined time over a standardised surface, agreed in advance. Football, rugby, hockey and all the major team games are played, at different venues around the world, to rules agreed by all participating national federations.

Canoe slalom is no exception. At the highest level, Olympic and world championship competition, there are agreed rules and procedures that are designed to produce fair, effective and meaningful competition, with the sole intention of ranking paddlers in order of their ability.

But canoe slalom has less **standardisation** than in some of these other sports. While football pitch sizes are standardised, and the distance over which a person will compete is known in advance in athletics, swimming and rowing, a canoe slalom course can vary significantly in its length and in the degree of difficulty. The issue is usually resolved for the major international slalom events because the start and finish points are agreed in advance and the course is approved by officials from the participating countries.

* * * *

My focus has always been the slalom course and its design. In the artificially created environment of canoe slalom, the course should be fundamental, not only at international level, but at **all levels**. The beginner needs to know what skills to acquire, what distances to prepare for, and the degree of difficulty he or she expects to face. It is this last point that continues to be ignored, and which has significant consequences for the sport. This is an even more important issue now that the minimum length restriction of boats has been removed. The balance between manoeuvrability and straight line speed is a factor that paddlers and course designers must now consider.

Each slalom in the lower divisions in Britain is designed by someone who is an 'experienced' paddler. There is no real alternative to this system because there is no effective 'slalom course designer' qualification. There is no meaningful standardisation of courses, and it is not possible to look at the majority of courses and determine whether a specific course is for division two, three, four or novice. We just **assume** the course is the right level for the division that is competing. The appropriateness of courses is assessed by the number of complaints, or lack of complaints. There is no requirement to include specific elements – except for the number of upstream gates. This is also true at international level. Team managers can only object to a gate if it is in a position which is deemed dangerous for the paddler, or potentially damaging to the boat. It is not possible to object on the grounds that the course is 'too easy', or fails to test the full range of skills that a paddler is expected to have in the different divisions.

In any other walk of life, where individuals are tested on their level of competence, there is a 'syllabus' to be covered, which states in detail the 'content' that might be included in the 'test'. Sports such as trampolining and gymnastics are very prescriptive in the elements that will be tested, but canoe slalom is not an appropriate sport for such control.

But – there **is** a problem that needs to be addressed. Without the guidance that a syllabus (of some kind) offers, the slalomist has difficulty organising a training programme to improve skill levels. Then, when the day of competition comes around, the 'course designer' has to cater for the paddler with lower skill levels, and does not have the same opportunities to extend the better performer. Inevitably the course is 'watered down'. Any other approach would be a big disincentive for any paddler who did not have the appropriate skill level to compete effectively. Such paddlers are likely to become disillusioned with the sport, and move to the growing world of 'playboaters' where **immediate** satisfaction is achieved by learning to perform progressively more difficult skills. Nobody in playboating **demands** a performer to perform a skill without giving him the opportunity to acquire that skill. The very informal environment of the playboater is more supportive to the inexperienced paddler than the whole world of slalom canoeing with its well organised structure of coaching support. One has only to look at the growth of new 'extreme' sports to appreciate the value of this argument.

At the other end of the scale, the better performer is not actively encouraged to raise his level of skill – because it will not be tested by the course designer. Instead, he will continue to focus on the basic elements of strength, speed and endurance. This is potentially a bigger problem. Sports where success is predominantly dependent on strength, speed and endurance, at the expense of skill, are on a continuous downward spiral in the UK. We stopped children under ten years of age working down the mines in the middle of the nineteenth century. They were being deprived of their childhoods, and suffered injuries through performing tasks that were inappropriate to their level of maturity and their physical and mental development. The practice of 'child labour' seems to have been revived. It is just the name that has changed from 'child labour' to children's elite sport'! It is not rocket science to study the increased weekly training demands for swimmers, runners and gymnasts that has occurred in the last ten years, and relate this to the increased demands that will occur in the next ten years. How much more training, and how many sacrifices will be needed in those sports that depend more on fitness and hard work than on talent, skill and judgment? More specifically, what would be the effect on the motivation of slalomists if the skill element was reduced and the strength, speed and endurance factors became even more important as determinants of success?

A couple of thousand years ago, the Greek philosopher, Plato, suggested that routine, mundane physical activity was for slaves, and not for 'freeborn' Greeks, and that physical activity should be a way of developing the mind through thinking and problem solving. Little has changed in his arguments – apart from the recognition that slavery is not an acceptable way to treat other people. The development of skill and understanding is individual to the human race. We can 'train' animals, like dogs and horses, to run fast, but we cannot get them to understand why! **Most** slalomists will never win any competitions, but get their satisfaction from mastery and control of their boat. They demonstrate competence in the same way that a club gymnast gets satisfaction from performing their first somersault unaided.

For all these reasons, the focus of slalom has to be mastery of the course and demonstration of skill. Strength, speed and endurance have to be subsidiary to this focus. Therefore, the sport has to decide which skills should be tested at **each** stage of paddler development. This will enable paddlers to prepare appropriately for a 'test' that is related to an 'expected' standard of performance. If the test is too simple, it does not discriminate according to level of **ability**, but on other factors such as strength, speed and endurance. If the test is too hard, or includes components that are not on the 'syllabus', the individual will not have had the opportunity to prepare adequately. It would, then, be an unfair 'test'. Furthermore, it could have a de-motivating effect on the paddler.

Only by graduated and staged progressions in slalom course design can we ensure the future development of the sport.

My era is over. There is much to do. All I can do is raise the issue.

* * * *

This has been an interesting project, where I have had time to reflect and revisit some of the most enjoyable and rewarding events of more than forty years as a coach in canoe slalom. Many of the people I met are now good friends. I have changed, but have tried to convey the thoughts that went through my mind at specific periods of time. Perhaps I have mellowed, and become more tolerant of those with whom I disagreed. As I move on, I am reminded of the words of James Joyce.

"I am a part of all that I have met,
Experience is an arch where through
Gleams the untravelled world
Forever and forever when I move."

I have much more travelling to do!

* * * *

ISBN 142510769-9

9 781425 107697